INVESTING
FOR
BEGINNERS

Which Investor Personality Type Are YOU? The Secret Guide to Selecting the Right Investment for Newbies - Stock Market, Forex, Options Trading, Futures, ETFs or Real Estate

BY

BENJAMIN WHITE

TABLE OF CONTENTS

INTRODUCTION

Investment is significant from numerous perspectives. Before investing, it is fundamental to comprehend what a venture is and its significance.

Investment is a demonstration of contributing cash to procure the benefit. It is the initial move towards the future security of your cash.

Investment: The need for it

The investment can help you later on whenever contributed carefully and appropriately. According to human instinct, we plan for a couple of days or think to get ready for the venture; however, we don't place the arrangement enthusiastically. Each individual must arrange for the venture and keep aside some measure of cash for what's to come. Most likely, what's to come is dubious, and it is required to contribute sagaciously with some specific arrangement of activities that can stay away from budgetary emergencies for the purpose of time. It can assist you in bringing a splendid and secure future. It gives you a secure future, yet besides, controls your spending design.

Significant Factors of Investments

Getting ready for Financial investment - Planning assumes an urgent job in all fields. For the money related venture, one must have a relevant arrangement by taking all ascent and fall circumstances of the market. You ought to have a decent learning of investment before making arrangements for money related ventures. Sharp perception and methodology are the essential requirements for effective monetary investment.

Contribute as indicated by your Needs and Capability-The reason behind the venture ought to be clear by which you can satisfy your needs from the investment. In venture, money related capacity is likewise a part that can bring you fulfillment and whatever outcomes you need. You can begin venture from a modest quantity according to your capacity. You should think about your salary and security to pick the best arrangement for you.

Investigate the market for accessible venture alternatives - The investment market is loaded with circumstances; you can investigate the market by applying the legitimate methodology. You can take help from money related organizers, administrators who have intensive information about interest in the market. Investigate the probability of investment markets and contact the wonderful tallness of progress by reasonable venture choices.

By taking assistance from an accomplished, capable monetary organizer and merchants can likewise give you the certainty to do well in the field of the venture. Presently the inquiry strikes the mind that what are the kinds of ventures?

Kinds of Investments

Common Funds-Basically, the shared reserve is an overseen venture support in which cash is destroyed from the financial specialists to purchase the protections.

Securities exchange

It is where different individuals exchange all-inclusive and acquire the greatest quantifiable profit. Nonetheless, it is fundamental to know the bull and bear of the securities exchange for putting resources into it. The Stock market for venture likewise incorporates the value market and clever market. You can put resources into values and clever market and get a great sum benefit by centered methodology and sharp examination of market pattern.

Bonds - It is the ideal approach to pick up enthusiasm on your chief sum. The intrigue and timeframe depend upon understanding. In this, holder loans a specific add up to the guarantor (borrower) for a fixed timeframe. As of now, you will get the enthusiasm from the borrower, and in the wake of finishing that fixed timeframe borrower will return back your cash. A long-haul device for money related ventures.

Fixed Deposits - The Fixed Deposit (FD) administration is given by different banks that offer speculators a higher pace of enthusiasm on their stores when contrasted with an ordinary investment account. Fixed stores have the development date to pick up the arrival on investment.

Land: One can likewise put resources into the land and manage the private and business property. This is likewise a slanting method to procure a decent quantifiable profit.

There are different money related organizers, budgetary supervisors, exchanging tips suppliers who can give you various choices for interest in the market. In any case, it is fundamental to pick the choices admirably.

We support investments that are easy, charge proficient, broadened, fluid, and straightforward. Numerous financial specialists regularly keep running into inconvenience when they put resources into things that don't have these five qualities. Ventures with these five qualities have been gainful after some time, however, they commonly are not energizing.

There is commonly not a "hot story that you have to follow up on now!" related to them. The monetary administration's industry, for the most part, doesn't support these kinds of investments since they produce next to no benefit from them. We are in the matter of boosting the abundance of our customers, not the budgetary administration's industry. Remember that this rundown of investment attributes isn't complete. Different components to search for in investments may incorporate appealing valuation, low relationship to your different possessions, a decent profit yield or premium pay, a tilt towards zones of the market that have created more significant yields, for example, esteem stocks, a proper hazard level for you, and so forth.

Minimal effort. We ordinarily put resources into the minimal effort, list-based assets and trade exchanged assets (ETF's). The assets we put resources to have a normal cost proportion of only 30% every year. The common effectively exchanged value shared store has a normal cost proportion of 1% or more. With venture reserves, the best indicator of future relative execution is the cost proportion on the store; the lower, the better. Speculative stock investments ordinarily have yearly cost proportions of 2% in addition to 20% of any benefits earned. Some factor annuities and lasting extra security "ventures" can have yearly costs of 2% or more. By watching out for the expenses of our ventures, we can spare our customers critical measures of cash every year and assist them with accomplishing better yields after some time (all else being equivalent). With venture items, you don't show signs of improvement execution with a greater expense item; in truth, you normally deteriorate execution.

Duty Efficient. Our investments (file-based assets and ETF's) are amazingly charged proficient, and they enable the financial specialist to have some power over the planning of the assessments. These sorts of assets have low turnover (exchanging movement), which is a typical trait of duty proficient investments. We suggest keeping away from shared assets with high turnover because of their duty wastefulness. After the ongoing huge increment in the U.S. financial exchange, numerous dynamic value common assets have "imbedded" capital increases of as much as 30%-45%. And when you purchase those shared subsidizes now, you may wind up covering capital additions government expenses on those embedded increases regardless of whether you didn't possess the reserve during the expansion. ETF's commonly don't produce long and momentary capital increase disseminations at year-end, and they don't have imbedded capital additions like dynamic shared assets. Speculative stock investments are normally charged wasteful because of their exceptionally high turnover. Notwithstanding putting resources into charge effective items we additionally accomplish numerous different things to help keep our customer assessments limited, for example, charge misfortune collecting, keeping our turnover/exchanging low, placing the correct sort of interests in the correct kind of records (charge area), utilizing misfortunes to counterbalance capital increases, utilizing possessions with huge capital additions for gifting, putting resources into tax-exempt city bonds, and so on.

We like to put resources into broadened reserves since they decrease your explicit stock hazard and the general danger of your portfolio. Awful news discharged around one stock may make it drop half, which is horrendous news if that stock is 20% of your entire portfolio, yet will be scarcely seen in a store of 1,000 stock positions. We will, in general, support finances that regularly have in any event a hundred properties and frequently a few hundred possessions or more. These enhanced subsidies give you an expansive portrayal of the entire resource class you are attempting to get an introduction to while taking out the explicit stock hazard. We are not liable to put resources into the freshest Solar Energy Company Equity Fund with 10 stock situations, for instance. We don't trust in going out on a limb (for example, explicit stock hazard) that you won't get paid for in higher anticipated return.

Basic. We lean toward investments that are

straightforward, straightforward, and straightforward. If you don't get it, don't put resources into it. The majority of our ventures are basic and straightforward; we know precisely what we claim. Convoluted venture items are structured for the dealer, not the purchaser, and ordinarily have high shrouded charges. Instances of confounded and non-straightforward ventures that we, for the most part, keep away from are flexible investments, private value reserves, organized items, some disaster protection "investment" items, variable annuities, privately owned business stock, new business stock or credits, and so on. Make everything as straightforward as could be allowed, however, not less complex.

We accept most financial specialists ought to have most of their portfolio put resources into things that have these five great attributes. By doing so, you will maintain a strategic distance from a lot of errors, negative astonishments, and dangers along the way. Moreover, we accept your after-assessment investment returns will probably be higher over extensive stretches of time. Obviously, few out of every odd shrewd or wise investment will have these attributes. For instance, salary delivering land property is illiquid (and regularly not differentiated) however, can be a fantastic long-haul venture whenever acquired and oversaw appropriately. Owning your very own business is illiquid and not expanded yet can be a great method to assemble riches also. We accept these five venture attributes become much progressively significant as you enter retirement, since by then, you might be increasingly centered on lessening hazard and safeguarding your riches than building it, and you may require the liquidity to spend and to bless some portion of your riches during retirement. These five incredible investment qualities can be a decent screening gadget for potential ventures and great components to consider when contributing.

CHAPTER 1

INVESTOR PERSONALITY TYPE

There are a few investigations of financial specialist types out there, so where do you start?

The CFA Institute breaks the character types into four primary gatherings: Preservers, Accumulators, Followers, and Independents. At that point, there's the notable Bailard, Biehl, and Kaiser (BB and K) five-way model, which depends on financial specialist certainty levels and their favored speculation strategy.

The Barnwell Two-Way Model* shows up superficially to be significantly more apparent, gathering financial specialists as either "uninvolved" or "dynamic." Each investigation has its benefits, albeit every one of the three could propose that an individual's sentiments towards hazard may change depending on the situation.

One critical thought when characterizing speculator character type is the equalization of the target (what you need to pick up and why) and requirements (time skyline, liquidity, and view of hazard). Likewise, are simply the assets you are contributing, your family, your business, or your customer.

A decent inquiry to pose would be, what amount does an individual's inclination towards hazard change if, for instance, you are an institutional financial specialist? Is it accurate to say that you are bound to take no chances for a superior possibility of ROI, or would your character overrule this for conceivable more significant yields yet on a higher bet?

Psychonomic Investor Profiling

The course of ordering financial specialist character types that we'll use here depends on Jonathan Myer's study. It holds that an individual's inclination towards hazard is probably not going to change, paying little mind to condition. Psychonomic financial specialist profiling instead recommends a speculator's sentiments towards risk could be shaded by how they see that specific hazard; this is notwithstanding how they feel about cash all in all, for example, regardless of whether it harms more to lose a pound than it does to increase a pound.

Speculator Personality Types

Mindful

Preservationist in speculation decisions, they have a substantial requirement for money related security and want to keep away from high hazard adventures. This kind of speculator is bound to confide in their financial information over that of an expert consultant.

They loathe losing even the scarcest measure of cash. As a result, any speculation choices require a lot of time, thought, and examination.

Passionate

This sort of speculator is bound to confide in the gut sense as opposed to doing intensive due perseverance; they put stock in karma or fortune. They contribute with their heart instead of the head, following a "hot tip" or whatever appears to be in trend.

This hopefulness and affinity to hold onto the day can be fulfilling. In any case, it can likewise prompt a hesitance to cut misfortunes on a terrible speculation choice with the expectation that things will work out inevitably.

Technical financial specialist character

Specialized speculators settle on their money related choices dependent on hard certainties and numbers.

They're screen-watchers, effectively exchanging on value variances and prepared to hurry should they recognize a pattern right off the bat. They can discover to compensate in their practice over the top perseverance and are continually searching for the edge with regards to the most recent tech advancements.

Occupied

As opposed to being occupied, think about investing. That character type lives for the buzz of the business sectors and exchanging. Continually checking the most recent value developments, they are frequently purchasing and selling dependent on the latest piece of tattle or prattle from papers and magazine stories.

But since of this profound aversion of dormancy, it can mean these financial specialists pass up a great opportunity by not waiting at a superior cost.

Easy-going

This kind of character is progressively laid back with regards to funding and speculation, in certainty, they're bound to be the one giving their assets over to an expert counselor to deal with things.

They accept there's more benefit to be found in a hard join than money related speculations. Subsequently, when they've made a venture, they're not liable to determine the status of how it's doing until they genuinely need to.

Educated

An educated speculator is one who uses data from numerous sources before settling on any monetary choices. They have a steady eye on venture advertisements just as the economy to work out what could give them a superior possibility of return.

They will cheerfully tune in to master guidance and read budgetary feelings, just conflicting with the market after careful thought of the considerable number of upsides and downsides. They have money related certainty and have faith in their options, believing that their insight and experience will convert into long haul gains.

Did you see yourself in any of the character types?

Regardless of whether any of the above sounded valid or was excessively treacherous, the most significant thing is this: Know thyself and know thy financial specialist qualities – and shortcomings.

Maybe you realize that your heart drives you when your head should, or perhaps when contributing assets in the interest of others, you're mindful of playing things excessively sheltered when you could be earning more noteworthy returns. In either case, utilizing a venture stage, you can trust, and that makes a substantial showing of due constancy, can have a significant effect on how you contribute and could improve your ROI.

Which financial specialist character best portrays you?

As indicated by the CFA Institute, there are four unique sorts of financial specialists dependent on particular conduct inclinations. The scope of these passionate and mental social predispositions assumes a job in how people contribute.

Other types include:

· Preservers

· Gatherers

· Supporters

· Independents

Preservers

Preservers are speculators who put a solid accentuation on monetary security and protecting their riches. They frequently fixate on momentary execution and misfortunes. Preservers much rather evade chance and experience issues making a move with their speculations. Furthermore, much the same as with contributing, this conduct of being conscious and careful is the way Preservers approach their work and individual lives.

Overwhelming Bias Type: Emotional, identifying with the dread of misfortunes and powerlessness to decide/make a move.

Significant Biases: Loss aversion and the state of affairs

Contributing Style: Wealth conservation first, development second

Level of Risk Tolerance: Generally lower than normal

Supporters

Supporters are financial specialists who are progressively inactive. They will, in general, pursue the lead of their companions and partners. Adherents will likewise seek the present contributing prevailing fashion. Frequently, their necessary leadership procedure doesn't include an extended haul plan. They have little enthusiasm for as well as have little inclination for contributing.

Prevailing Bias Type: Cognitive, identifying with the following the conduct

Significant Biases: Recency and surrounding

Contributing Style: Passive

Level of Risk Tolerance: Generally lower than usual however regularly thinks hazard resilience level is higher than it is

Independents

Mentality: One should say I have set aside the effort to comprehend the speculation I intend to make, regardless of whether I pass up on chances like this.

Independents are financial specialists who are diagnostic, essential scholars. They have unique thoughts regarding contributing and need to be effectively associated with the speculation procedure. They are happy to go out on a limb and adhere to a venture intend to achieve their money related objectives. Independents will, in general, be masterminds and practitioners rather than devotees and visionaries.

Overwhelming Bias Type: Cognitive, identifying with the traps of doing one's very own examination

Active Biases: Confirmation and accessibility

Contributing Style: Active

Level of Risk Tolerance: Generally better than expected yet not as high as forceful financial specialists

Gatherers

Attitude: I should act rapidly on chances to profit.

Collectors are financial specialists who are keen on amassing riches. They like to be vigorously required by changing their portfolio assignments and possessions to economic situations and may not wish to pursue an organized arrangement. Collectors are daring individuals and are firm adherents that whatever way they pick is the right one.

Predominant Bias Type: Emotional, identifying with presumptuousness and want for impact over venture process

Useful Biases: Overconfidence and figment of control

Contributing Style: Actively occupied with essential leadership

Level of Risk Tolerance: High to exceptionally high

CHAPTER 2

FOREX TRADING: A BEGINNER'S GUIDE

The forex market is the world's most significant global cash exchanging business sector, working relentlessly during the working week. Most forex exchanging is finished by experts, for example, financiers. By and substantial forex exchanging is done through a forex intermediary - however, there is nothing to stop anybody transferring monetary forms. Forex cash exchanging enables purchasers and merchants to purchase the money they require for their business and venders who have earned money to trade what they have for progressively helpful money. The world's biggest banks rule forex. As indicated by a review in The Wall Street Journal Europe, the ten most dynamic merchants who are occupied with forex exchanging represent practically 73% of exchanging volume.

Since the business sectors for monetary forms are worldwide, the volumes exchanged each day are tremendous. For the huge corporate speculators, the incredible advantages of exchanging on Forex are:

Tremendous liquidity - over $4 trillion every day, which is $4,000,000,000. It implies there's consistently somebody prepared to exchange with you

All of the world's free monetary forms tare exchanged - this implies you may transfer the cash you need whenever

Twenty four - hour exchanging during the 5-day working week

Tasks are worldwide which imply that you can exchange with any piece of the world whenever

From the perspective of the littler broker, there are loads of advantages as well, for example:

A quickly changing business sector - that is one which is continually evolving and offering the opportunity to profit

All around created instruments for controlling danger

The capacity to go long or short - this implies you can profit either in rising or falling markets

Influence exchanging - implying that you can profit by huge volume exchanging while at the same time having a generally low capital base

Heaps of alternatives for zero-commission exchanging

How the forex Market Works

As forex is about foreign trade, all exchanges are made up of a money pair - state, for example, the Euro and the US Dollar. The essential instrument for exchanging forex is the conversion scale, which is communicated as a proportion between the estimations of the two monetary forms, for example, EUR/USD = 1.4086. This worth, which is alluded to as the 'forex rate' implies that, at that specific time, one Euro would be worth 1.4086 US Dollars. And this proportion is continuously communicated to 4 decimal spots, which indicate that you could see a forex pace of EUR/USD = 1.4086 or EUR/USD = 1.4087 yet never EUR/USD = 1.40865. So, the furthest right digit of this proportion is alluded to as a 'pip.' Thus, a change from EUR/USD = 1.4086 to EUR/USD = 1.4088 would result in a difference in 2 pips. One pip, in exchange and this manner, is the littlest unit.

With a forex rate at EUR/USD = 1.4086, a speculator buying 1000 Euros and using dollars would pay $1,408.60. The forex rate at that point shifted to EUR/USD = 1.5020; we can say that the speculator could sell their 1000 Euros for $1,502.00 and bank the $93.40 as a benefit. If this doesn't appear to be enormous, add up to you, you need to place the entirety into the setting. With a falling or rising business sector, the forex rate doesn't just change uniformly, yet sways and benefits can be taken all the time as a price wavers around a pattern.

When you're expecting the worth EUR/USD to fall, you may exchange the other route by selling Euros for Dollars and repurchasing then when the forex rate has changed to further your potential benefit.

How Risky is Forex?

Whenever you exchange on forex as in any cash exchanging, you're in the matter of money hypothesis, and it is only that - theory. It implies there is some hazard associated with forex money trading as in any business; however, you may and should find a way to limit this. You can generally set a point of confinement to the drawback of any exchange, that way, to characterize the most extreme misfortune that you are set up to acknowledge whether the market conflicts with you - and it will focus on events.

The best protection against losing your shirt on the forex market is to decide to comprehend what you're doing completely. Quest the web for decent forex exchanging instructional exercise and study it in detail-a touch of proper forex training can go far!. At the point when there are bits you don't comprehend, search for decent forex exchanging gathering and pose parts and heaps of inquiries. A large number of the individuals who routinely answer your questions on this will have proper forex exchanging online journals, and this will likely offer you responses to your inquiries as well as give heaps of connects to great destinations. Be cautious; in any case, look out for forex exchanging tricks. Try not to rush to part with your cash and research anything very well before you shell out any well-deserved!

The Forex Trading Systems

While you might be directly in being wary about any forex exchanging framework that it's publicized, there are some great ones around. A large portion of them either use forex graphs and by methods for these, recognize forex exchanging signals which advise the dealer when to purchase or sell. This sign comprises of a specific change in a forex rate or a pattern, and these will have been concocted by a forex dealer who has concentrated long haul inclines in the market to distinguish substantial sign when they happen. A significant number of the frameworks will utilize forex exchanging programming, which recognizes such hedge from information inputs that are assembled naturally from market data sources. Some use mechanized forex exchanging programming, which can trigger exchanges consequently when the sign tells it to do as such. And when these sound unrealistic to you, search for online forex exchanging frameworks that will permit you to embrace some fake exchanging to test them out. So, by doing this, you can get some forex trading preparation by giving them a turn before you put genuine cash on the table.

So, How Much do you Need to Start?

Be aware that this is a bit of a 'How long is a piece of string?' question. However, there are ways to be a beginner to start. Be also aware that the minimum trading size for most trades on forex is usually 100,000 units of any currency. This volume is known as a standard "lot." Meanwhile, numerous organizations offer the office to buy in drastically littler parts than this, and a touch of web looking through will before long find these. Various adverts are citing just two or three hundred dollars to get moving! You will regularly observe the term acciones exchanging forex, and this is only a general term that covers the little person trading forex. Short scale transferring offices, for example, these are frequently called as forex smaller than usual exchanging.

Where do You Start?

The absolute most evident answer is obviously - on the web! Online forex exchanging gives you direct access to the Forex showcase, and there are parcels and bunches of organizations out there who are good to go to manage you on the web. Be cautious, do invest the energy to get some in order high forex exchanging training, again this can be given on the internet and set up your spurious record to trade before you endeavor to go live. Whenever you do well and take as much time as is needed, there's no motivation behind why you shouldn't be effective in forex exchanging along these lines, have persistence and stick at it!

As a rule, the time between the give up and opening function is short and endures just solely minutes. Benefits picked up from this role will in accepted below. Be that as it may, the all-out make bigger finished by using gigantic positions can be noteworthy. Some Forex brokers trade up to 200 conditions in a day. Indeed, no longer all posts opened by using dealers can make advantages for them, yet the decisive goal is to have a typical gain by becoming a member of all positions.

One tip is that when scalping, you should post a stop-misfortune request extremely close to the opening price of the scenario for decreasing the misfortunes when there is variance toward the market. It is regularly recommended that you utilize a stop-misfortune on your scalping exchanges. As this is one of the stepped forward Forex exchanging strategies, how about we abridge this methodology and the tips a supplier ought to consent to:

• Don't preserve a role open for too long; ideally, the most excessive keeping time ought now not to surpass five minutes.

• The size of the trade ought to be pretty huge, as the measure of picked up pips per exchange is very little.

• The higher the extent of the day by way of day exchanges is, the higher the odds are of being fruitful with Forex scalping.

• This machine is official for informal investors, implying that you would most presumably need to invest a high-quality deal of energy changing to accomplish effects with it.

Positional Trading

This is positively a progressed Forex technique, as it is utilized by way of the top-acquiring dealers. The preferred imperative function of this system is that it requires notably much less everyday consideration. In any case, it has to be completed effectively with a cautious lengthy haul show off the investigation. Most Forex changing structures are carried out on little league outlines, implying that most of them are day exchanging procedures.

Positional replacing is something no longer quite the same as day replacing – and it's in particular not the same as scalping. At the factor when a provider starts exchanging positions, they are relied upon to preserve a scenario for a severe vast stretch. It is difficult to distinguish the base suggested keeping time as it mainly relies upon the dealer's diagram of the market, and the number of pips picked up.

When utilizing positional exchanging, one of the most progressive Forex strategies, a dealer wishes to do the whole thing in totally the contrary route contrasted with Forex scalping; the other measurement will in ordinary be relatively little in correlation with the exchanging capital. While scalping, you exercise to open sizable situations, as you are hoping to make a couple of pips for every exchange. During positional exchanging, you intend to get more than 100 pips, which can make your role higher impenetrable when the market vacillates.

Technical strategy

Technical analysis is essential when buying and selling Forex or any different asset. The fundamentals would possibly set the path of a pair, but the professional evaluation dictates the entry and exit tiers of your trades. If you pass by the technicals, you may also give up dropping even if your assessment is impeccable. So, FX Leaders continuously update its technical Forex techniques to replicate the altering market stipulations and assist you in becoming aware of exact entry and exit points, as nicely as how to manage yourself when in a trade.

Fibonacci Indicator – Forex Trading Strategies

The Fibonacci buying and selling approach is one of the most customary and, in many instances, used long-term technical techniques on the Forex. It tries to location charge motion in the desirable context by the usage of the Fibonacci sequence, a close illustration of the historical "Golden Ratio." Fibonacci numbers are no longer solely frequently used in the economic markets but are additionally utilized to physics, geometry, engineering, and art.

Regarding Forex trading, there are many makes use of this particular mathematical construct. This unique Fibonacci trading approach is dependent on a phenomenon called a "pullback." To wholly apprehend how pullbacks work, we ought to first discuss a more critical thought — the trend.

A style is genuinely a directional go in rate over a defined period. When looking at every rate alternate individually, it can be a challenge to find an excellent pattern. However, through searching at the larger picture, traits are effortlessly identifiable. Spotting a strong trend is a necessary section of imposing a Fibonacci trading strategy. Without the presence of a trend, this approach is of limited effectiveness and impact.

Breaking Down The Fibonacci Trading Strategy

The picture above demonstrates a decently short pattern, which is the sort of design that we will concentrate on when separating this specific Fibonacci exchanging methodology. The trend comprises of three legs: two going up and one going down.

Since the general bearing of the pattern is up, the center part, where there is a fleeting ruin, is known as a "pullback." The issue with recognizing pullbacks is that when we see a pattern begin to switch, it is complicated to understand a withdrawal from an inversion of the design. It is the place the Fibonacci exchanging system comes in. The method enables us to break down the information, assess value activity, and specialty an official conclusion.

Fibonacci numbers and proportions have been acclaimed among mathematicians and artisans for a long time. They are found much of the time all through nature and, when applied to the monetary markets, can work as extraordinary explanatory apparatuses. No math is required to utilize these numbers — the product exchanging stages play out every vital figure for us. By and by, executing a Fibonacci trading methodology Forex is direct and intuitive. The principal undertaking that we should finish is to settle on a choice dependent on the lines which show up on the chart.

Applying The Fibonacci Sequence

On the graph over, the Fibonacci proportions are the purple lines drawn evenly. They speak to the 38.2%,

50.0%, and 61.8% retracements of the predominant upturn. By looking at how far the pullback has come to on the Fibonacci scale, we can decide two things: regardless of whether the cost will resume to the bull or turn around into a crisp bearish pattern. In any case, we can arrange to exchange every potential situation.

The general Fibonacci exchanging methodology standard expresses that as long as the value stays over the 61.8% line, we can anticipate that the pattern should proceed. It shows the bearish value activity is just a pullback, not an out and out inversion. On the other side, when the value crosses the 61.8% line, we should regard it as the beginning of a bearish pattern. And when we are long this market, the time has come to finish off and proceed onward to the following exchange.

Investigation

The diagram above delineates a pullback that structures a base at around the half Fibonacci marker. It shows the cost will in all likelihood rise, and the general upward pattern will proceed. As per this reality, we can modify our exchange of the board appropriately. If we are long this market, at that point holding the position is legitimate exchange the executives' methodology. If we are searching for a short section, at that point, hanging tight for a better exchange area is the play.

In any case, the utilization of the Fibonacci grouping has given us a solid structure for making position the executive's views on-the-fly. We are currently ready to routinely recognize our optimal assume benefit and stop misfortune value levels. With this data, we can offset chance with remuneration and expand or compensate while restricting danger.

Even Levels – Forex Trading Strategies

Even Levels is one of the least complex yet fantastically helpful thoughts in Forex exchanging. Low levels are significant in most Forex trading techniques and help us in dissecting outlines. So, in any case, they can likewise be made use of individually as a procedure as opposed to only a device for different techniques. By viewing the most explicit value changes and drawing their low levels, we can make fruitful exchanges. In thoroughly understanding the flat degrees of increasingly complex outlines, we can spot slants that we would have generally missed.

The significance of flat levels

Most merchants believe low levels to be similarly as significant as value activity, which is the center to Forex exchanging. Dissecting the blend of the value change and the low levels can enable us to comprehend the pattern and foresee where the market will go straight away. Albeit even levels are an exceptionally fundamental Forex exchanging technique, numerous renowned and experienced dealers, for example, Jesse Livermore, Warren Buffett, and George Soros, have affirmed that they use it as a premise to a large number of their systems.

Low levels help us spot key zones on a diagram where an adjustment in the pattern is probably going to happen. This can help us when choosing where to put a stop, or when we need to enter an exchange yet don't have a clue about the correct time to do as such. Exact planning can be critical in numerous Forex exchanging techniques, and a careful investigation of the even levels can enable us to locate the right planning and spot a decent exchange. Remember that even levels might be the establishment for some techniques; however, all alone, it usually is insufficient and must be utilized in blend with other Forex exchanging methodologies.

Even Levels and 'Swing Points'

The ideal approach to utilize even levels furthering our potential benefit is by breaking down the swing focuses. Swing focuses are focuses on where the pattern changes, and by stamping even levels at these focuses, we can see costs where it is likely as an adjustment in a model. The outline beneath unmistakably indicates how we can utilize even levels our potential benefit.

low the swing focuses tend to rehash themselves. Bolster levels can transform into obstruction levels and the other way around. By denoting the low levels on the graph, we can anticipate when the following swing point will happen and enter/leave an exchange at the ideal time. The circles on the diagram are the focuses that we ought to have had the option to see in cutting edge. These are the clearest passage focuses, and by seeing them, we would have given an edge to any methodology that we utilized.

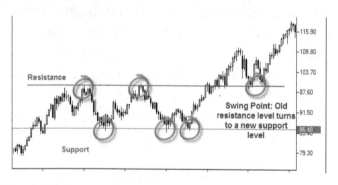

Horizontal Levels and Ranging Markets

Parallel ranges are also beneficial in range-bound markets. Range-bound markets are markets where the rate has evident upper and decrease boundaries that the charge doesn't cross. By observing the cost as it processes one of the limitations, we can predict with tremendous accuracy where the fee will fashion next.

As always, the fee can be unpredictable and might smash the boundary just as we determine to enter a trade, but overall, this approach is very reliable and safe.

Head and Shoulders – Forex Trading Strategies

As we have already talked about 'Candlestick Trading Strategy', which permits us to recognize the candlestick charts and what every candlestick indicates. However, in reality, grow to be a master of the charts, we ought to study a few frequent chart patterns and what information we can draw from them about the future.

So, the 'head and shoulders' pattern is one of many recognizable and tradable chart patterns. In Forex jargon, they are acknowledged as "shampoo" due to the fact of the shampoo company of the equal name. The Head and shoulders Forex patterns consist of an excessive height in the middle and two double peaks on both facets of that one, as can be viewed in the illustration below. The higher height is the head, and the two decrease ones are the shoulders. The pattern itself appears like a head between two joints. As a result, the name.

Head And Shoulders Trading

Head and shoulders patterns emerge as applicable

when the neckline is penetrated. Once the neckline is broken, we may additionally seem to be to open a brief function on the contrary aspect of the head and shoulders buying and selling indicator.

Some merchants enter immediately, while others prefer to come on a pullback and retest of the neckline. The latter alternative is safer because now we recognize that this is now not just a fake-out. The range of pips targeted in this method is identical to the wide variety of pips between the top of the head and the neckline. So, when the market is feeling right, and there is extra room to go after attaining the target, we may aim for higher earnings and let the exchange run.

Head And Shoulders Forex Pattern: A Typical Candlestick Chart

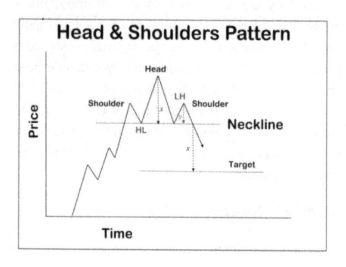

This picture above is apparent and allows for precise attention of the head and shoulders trading pattern. Don't count on the actual charts to be as clean — they will supply extra of a challenge. To change these patterns, we have to spot them in real-time as they happen, no longer after they are irrelevant.

The bottom line, usually referred to as the neckline, is a guide level. It might also now not continually be a straight line, but an ascending or descending sequence. The slope element to the neckline makes it a whole lot extra hard to spot; thus, we ought to center of attention on the larger picture. Junior traders must likely switch to a line chart, which makes some patterns extra visible, as an alternative of the candle chart. The photograph below is a real chart displaying a head and shoulders Forex pattern. Recognizing the head and shoulders trading sample in real-time and buying and selling it efficaciously is a great deal extra tricky than shown here in the illustrations.

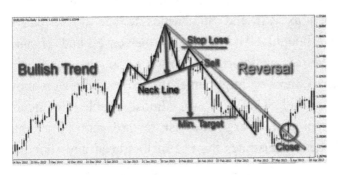

Spotting Head And Shoulders Forex Patterns

As cited above, the neckline should be damaged for the head and shoulders pattern to be usable. Nonetheless, real-life trading doesn't follow textbook guidelines so strictly. We have to be smart and flexible to spot these patterns as they are forming, to minimize the danger and maximize the profits.

One trick for early pattern cognizance and coming into high chance prevailing trades is to look at the volumes. No count number the time frame; the amount is supposed to decrease with each peak. And of course, as with most things trading, this isn't always the case. The reduced volume on the 2d height, which is the head, means that customers had an attempt on the upside, but besides a great deal force. As a result, the rate subsequently goes down.

So, when we are at the top of the 2nd shoulder and quantity is low, we need to check different symptoms such as RSI and Stochastics to see if the pair is overbought. And if that's the case, and if pins, inverted hammers are forming on the candlestick chart, then we might enter the trade with a stop above the head. This way, we almost double the income target and enlarge the risk-reward ratio. The chart beneath illustrates the use of this head and shoulders trading strategy but on an ascending pattern.

The volume Decreases With Every Peak.

Inverse Head And Shoulders

'Backwards Head and Shoulders' examples are something contrary to head and shoulders. All principles apply. However, they are topsy-turvy. For this situation, the neck area additionally fills in as obstruction. It implies we should hope to purchase upon the break of the neck area. Like head and shoulders, they might be straight, climbing, or sliding.

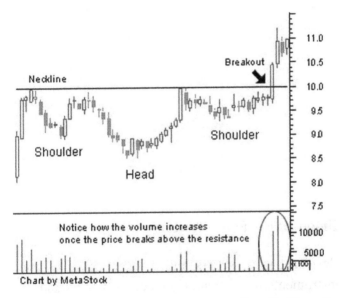

Chart by MetaStock

Opposite Head And Shoulders Trading Is Exactly The Same But Upside-Down.

Head and shoulders examples are not a Forex exchanging technique all alone. In any case, they do assist us with getting a superior picture of what is happening and what will occur straightaway. Having the option to detect these examples can be the distinction between a triumphant exchange and a losing one.

As you acquire understanding as a broker, have a go at fusing whatever number of these procedures into your exchanging system bin as could reasonably be expected. Likely outcomes are improved execution and a chance to get more cash-flow.

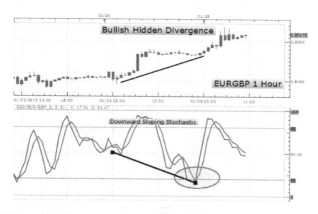

Uniqueness – Forex Trading Strategies

Besides basics, sellers and analysts of cash related instruments use different pointers to understand what may come to pass for the expense of a particular tool. These pointers offer a central system for seeing plans and envisioning what course the cost will slant.

For the most part, these pointers are what makes Forex

signals possible. They consider a total steady assessment of significant worth action, and the gathering here at FX Leaders realizes them on a regular reason.

What Is Divergence?

Dissimilarity is a primary marker used by our professionals at FX Leaders to assist increase benefits. The chance of entering the market at the opportune time the correct way increments on every occasion utilized related to different pointers, for example, Moving Averages (MA), RSI, Stochastics, or distinctive assist and opposition levels.

What Is Divergence Trading?

By genuinely recognizing the title "difference," one can without an awful lot of a stretch tell that uniqueness replacing is a type exchanging mounted in disharmony or deviation. Disparity Forex exchanging methods are as frequently as feasible utilized with the aid of cash dealers around the world.

In principle, expenses and pointers have to go a similar way at equal rates. On the off danger that the value arrives at a higher high, at that factor, the marker has to arrive at a more significant high. On the off threat that the benefit comes at a decrease steep, at that factor, the pointer needs to go with the identical pattern. The equal applies to lower lows and higher lows.

In the match that the fee and the related pointers don't associate, at that point, you can tell that some progress is going to happen. The excellent markers to use in dissimilarity changing are Stochastics, RSI, MACD, and Trade Volume.

A bullish distinction occurs when the award in the marker is extra advantageous than the difference in the price — bearish disparity is a unique way. While applying this differentiation, there are four indispensable sorts of dissimilarity:

• Regular Bullish

• Hidden Bullish

• Regular Bearish

• Hidden Bearish

We will make clear every kind and how to trade the concerning disparity Forex procedure.

Regular Bullish

Standard divergences are utilized as an apparatus to exhibit inversions. This EUR/USD month to month outline demonstrates the fee of making a decrease low for two days. In any case, the energy in MACD and Stochastics didn't relate to that of the cost activity, making higher lows. This hedge a possible inversion of the sample or perchance a comply with the downtrend or something similar.

'In reverse Head and Shoulders' models are something in opposition to head and shoulders. All standards apply, anyway they are essential upside down. For this circumstance, the neck zone furthermore fills in as an obstacle. It infers we should plan to buy upon the break of the neck zone. Like head and shoulders, they may be straight, climbing, or sliding.

Regular Bearish

As we can see from the USD/CHF chart, the price reached a high in the previous week and then made a higher high the following week. On the other hand, the MACD indicator at the bottom of the chart is making lower highs. This is called 'Regular Bearish Divergence' and indicates a fall in the price to come.

In this case, since we are in an uptrend, we should expect a retracement. After entering at the top, we should look to get out of the trade at the uptrend line.

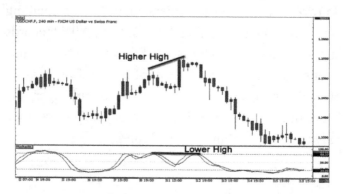

Regular Bearish Divergence – The price is making higher highs while MACD is making lower highs.

Unlike regular divergence, hidden divergence indicates a continuation of the trend. This EUR/USD chart shows the occasion where the price was making higher lows, while the stochastic was making lower lows. This divergence indicates that the retrace down is over, and trend continuation is about to resume.

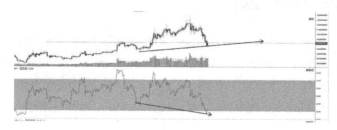

Hidden Bullish Divergence – unlike regular divergence, hidden divergence indicates the continuation of the trend.

Hidden Bearish

The daily EUR/USD chart below gives a clear example of hidden divergence and the trend reversal that follows. We can see that when stochastic was nearing overbought levels and had established separation with the price, which made lower highs, the pair fell immediately and began a downtrend. This sort of chart pattern means that when the stochastic was overbought the second time, EUR/USD buyers couldn't push any higher. So, the upside was complete even though EUR/USD couldn't make new highs. This is a bearish reversing signal.

Hidden Bearish Divergence – when Stochastics are nearing overbought levels, the pair falls immediately to continue the downtrend.

When Using Divergence Forex Strategies

Divergence is quite easy to spot, as it only requires drawing a few lines. Nonetheless, sometimes we look too hard at the charts. This makes us see things that aren't there.

During periods of consolidation or low liquidity, small divergences between price and indicators might form — but that doesn't mean we should consider them real discrepancies. The chart below shows a four-day consolidation period with symbols, and the price does not correlate accurately. However, this setup does not constitute a divergence.

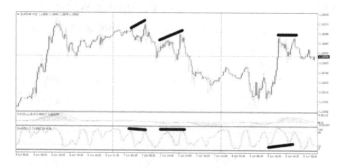

In union periods, not everything that resembles difference is dissimilarity — be cautious.

Dissimilarity is probably an ideal approach to utilize pointers to examine diagrams. Close by other help and obstruction techniques, the uniqueness Forex exchanging can be used to give your diagnostic aptitudes the push they have to make you a genuinely gainful broker. And when you need to discover how disparity exchanging is utilized in live market circumstances, investigate our week after week examination from April 17-23. In our week by week investigation, our top Forex specialists clarify how they use uniqueness exchanging, close by other Forex systems to dissect the market's activities consistently.

Candle Strategy in Forex

Neither one of the candlesticks examples can be an exchanging signal itself, nor would it be able to be utilized for a showing of the potential sections. The model demonstrates the desires in the market and signalizes the possible changes. For looking for the passage, another technique for examination, as opposed to candles, ought to be utilized.

If you lean toward day exchanging, being doubtful to pointers, at that point Japanese candle Forex exchanging system would live up to your desires. Candle examples empower a broker to decide the market circumstance just as organic market balance.

Characteristics of the candle design investigation

The more extended the «body» of the candle in Forex, the more grounded the Momentum and the more prominent the possibility to move in the indicated bearing. A bullish candle with the enormous body and the short shade demonstrates that the purchasers impact the market more than the dealers. A «bearish» flame with the colossal body and quick «shade» implies that the market supply is more grounded than interest. A long «shade» explicit way suggests that during the time spent the candle's arrangement in Forex; the organic market parity has moved. The progressions of the market desires can be dictated by contrasting the candles and one another.

The little shade from either side demonstrates more prominent odds of the development distinct way. Generally equivalent «shades» gave the candle's body is little (Doji candles for Forex design) speaks to advertise uncertainty - the weight on the purchaser's and dealer's cost is around the equivalent. In such conditions, even a little development in volume of exchange may cause a stable value development; all the more regularly, there is a pattern to switch.

The principle candle exchanging frameworks:

The candle designs which might be characterized as inversion examples caution about inversion pattern as well as about the parallel development start or exit from it; and now and then about decrease of the development's speed without altering of the course. Any example bodes well just where it arrives at the most grounded level. If an inversion example succeeds, at that point, it will be trailed by constant distinct development.

All exchanging examples made up of 1-2 candles would lose their importance if, during current development (pattern or revision in value development), this example applied more than once. This is particularly valid for Doji candle designs. The most dependable Japanese candle sign shows up on the Daily period. Following time allotment decline, the unwavering quality of the sign brings down.

A case of exchanging candles technique dependent on Engulfing design

Candle Forex exchanging system utilizes this candle design as an inversion signal or the revision starts.

Trading asset: It is any currency pair.

Trading period: This is the European and sessions.

Timeframe: This usually D1 or H1.

Candlestick trading strategy for a signal to buy:

The development of a candle «engulfing» example is required on the low of the descending pattern.

The sign is affirmed: it tends to be a Doji candle example or one all the more Engulfing case a similar way.

Low of the first Engulfing example must not be recharged; in addition - the more remote the value, the more grounded an exchanging signal.

Right now of the following candle opening, we will open a long position. Stop Loss will be fixed underneath a Low affirmation sign.

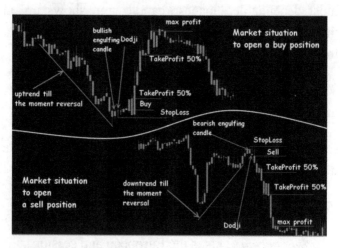

Candlestick strategy Forex for the signal to sell:

The development of the candle «engulfing» example is required on the high of the upward pattern.

The sign is affirmed: Doji candle example or one all the more Engulfing case a similar way.

High of the first Engulfing example must not be recharged.

We will open a short position right now of the

following candle arrangement. Stop Loss will be set over the High affirmation signal.

The candle Forex methodology with «Free candle» pointer

The exchanging methodology utilizes candle designs with a high unwavering quality level and sliding standard for the assurance of the present pattern. EMA(9) is prompted for the famous money pair exchanging on the M15 period. «Free candle» is viewed as a full-fledged 15-minute flame, body, and shade of which don't contact the EMA (9) line, and the end cost of the candles in Forex exchanging isn't higher/bring down the past outrageous. «Free candle» must have the typical «body» and regular «shade» («hammer,» «dodgy» inversion examples, and GAP are not relevant).

I am exchanging resources: EUR/USD, USD/JPY, USD/CHF, GBP/USD, EUR/GBP, EUR/JPY, GBP/JPY.

I am exchanging period: the European and the US exchanging session. Candle Forex exchanging the times of the market's uncertainty isn't fitting.

The fundamental pattern's heading is dictated by EMA(9). For the extended position (purchase), the presence of the «free» bullish flame above EMA(9) is required. The rear light's entrance after «free candle» or a Buy Stop request ought to be somewhat higher than the end cost. The Stop Loss is fixed at the maximum level of the free candle.

And for a short position (sell), a «free bearish candle» ought to be fixed underneath the moving normal. The section at the opening of the following flame relies upon the market or ought to be made by a pending Sell Stop request. A Stop Loss ought to be fixed 3-5 beneath min of the «free light.

For the setting of Taking Profit, two scopes of the free light ought to be used.

A decent minute for the section with regards to candle system exchanging respect to first cash sets shows up inside 15-30 minutes after the European session opening when the market bearing has been resolved. The standard length of the open arrangement is as long as 60 minutes. It isn't prescribed to exchange without Stop Loss or enter inside initial 5 minutes of every hour.

The arrangement ought to be opened except if:

good ways from shutting cost of the «free candle» to EMA(9) is under 3-4;

The body of the «free candle» is under 10.

From the scientific desire planned, the «free candle» Forex candle exchanging is adequately viable, if the arrangements are not made time after time and just in dependable designs.

Ascending Triangle Pattern

This triangle example has its upper side level and the lower one climbing. As such, the highest points of this triangle are on a similar level, and the bottoms are expanding. This sort of triangle regularly has a bullish character. When you recognize this triangle on the outline, you ought to be set up to catch a bullish value move equivalent to in any event the size of the triangle. As such, breakouts through the upper level (the level side) is utilized for setting section focuses for long positions. This is a sketch of the rising triangle outline design:

The dark lines above show the value activity inside the triangle development. The blue lines allude to the sides of the triangle, which contains the value activity. The red lines relate to the size of the triangle and its potential objective, which is commonly a 1:1 estimated move. At the point when an ascending triangle is framed during a bullish pattern, we anticipate a continuation of the design.

Diving Triangle Pattern

As noted before, the climbing and slipping triangles are an equal representation of one another. In that capacity, the sliding triangle example has the contrary trademark. The flat side of the sliding triangle is underneath the value activity. The upper side of the triangle is slanted downwards. In a bearish market, the plunging triangle has a bearish potential equivalent to in any event the size of the example. Thus, the sliding triangle is utilized to open short positions after the cost has broken its lower (level) side. How about we see the sketch of the slipping triangle:

At the point when the dropping triangle is made during a bearish value propensity, we anticipate that the pattern should proceed.

It is essential to refer to that the rising and the plunging triangles some of the time get through the slanted level, causing false hedge and catching a few merchants en route. Similar remains constant at the level cost zone. You ought to consistently attempt to sit tight for the end of the flame to affirm the breakout. This will help lessen a significant number of the bogus sign.

Rising/Falling Wedge

The rising and falling wedges are like the mounting and the sliding triangle designs. Notwithstanding, the rising and the falling wedges have no flat side. The two sides of the prongs are inclining a similar way. We should portray the two sorts of wedges you will discover on the value outline.

Rising Wedge

This is a triangle diagram design, where the two sides are slanted upwards. The value makes higher tops and considerably higher bottoms. This makes the two rising lines collaborate, creating a kind of triangle design on the diagram. The rising wedge has a solid bearish character. As such, the trigger side of the wedge example is the lower line. When you recognize a breakout through the lower level of a rising wedge, you ought to expect a sharp value drop equivalent to at any rate the size of the example. In this manner, breakouts through the lower level of a wedge are utilized for opening short positions. Itis what the rising wedge arrangement resembles:

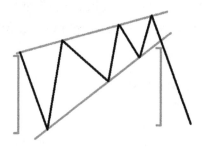

Falling Wedge

With the falling wedge design, the two sides are slanted downwards. The value makes lower bottoms and even lower tops. This way, the different sides of the triangle are sliding and agreement to a sharp point. Inverse to the rising wedge, the falling wedge has a solid bullish character. In this way, the trigger side of the falling wedge arrangement is the upper line. At the point when the value breaks the top degree of a falling wedge, you should go for a bullish move at any rate as tremendous as your wedge arrangement. Brokers utilize the falling wedge to set a long section that focuses on the graph. Underneath you will see a sketch of a falling wedge:

Since you recognize what the rising and the falling wedges appear as though we should share one more insight into these developments. Wedges could have pattern continuation, or pattern inversion character. At the point when the wedge shows up after an all-encompassing value move, we anticipate an inversion of the pattern, when the wedge shows up prior in the design, we expect that it should be an impermanent retracement that will proceed with the principle model set up. Ordinarily, the more dominant wedge development is the potential pattern inversion arrangement, which happens after a delayed pattern move.

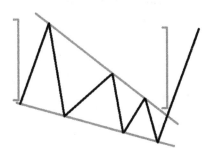

Symmetrical Triangle Pattern

The even triangle is a circumstance on the graph where the highest points of the value activity are lower, and the bottoms are higher. Additionally, the different sides of the triangle are slanted with a similar point. This makes the balanced character of the triangle.

Ordinarily, with balanced triangle design, the normal directional breakout is obscure. The purpose behind this is bullish, and the bearish move has equivalent quality as observed through the value activity.

At the point when a breakout in the end happens, it is probably going to incite a value move equivalent to the size of the example. In this manner, you ought to deliberately distinguish a potential breakout in the upper and the lower level of the balanced triangle to take the exact situation in the market. The sketch underneath shows the equitable triangle development and conceivable breakout situations:

As you see from the model over, the potential objective depends on the size of the triangle development. With this kind of estimated move investigation, you will realize what's in store from the balanced triangle breakout, regardless of whether it breaks upwards, or downwards.

Hedges

Hedges on the diagram have a comparable shape to that of even triangles. They normally show up during patterns and have a pattern continuation character.

Bullish Pennant

The bullish pennant is like a balanced triangle in appearance, yet the Bullish hedge arrangement comes after a cost increment. Since hedges have pattern continuation character, the bullish hedge is probably going to proceed with the bullish pattern on the graph. At the point when the upper side of the hedge gets broken upwards, we are probably going to see an expansion equivalent to at any rate the size of the hedge, and normally bigger.

Thus when exchanging hedges, a subsequent objective ought to likewise be utilized to get a more significant move. When figuring the following goal, you would break down the value leg promptly following the hedge. You could set the objective to 1:1 of the past leg or .618 of that leg. At the point when the pattern appears to be stable and has a lofty slant, a 1:1 estimated move would be a suitable second target, and in every other case, the .618 of the leg could be utilized. How about we investigate the bullish hedge underneath:

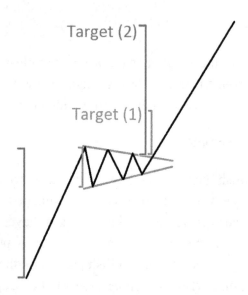

See that here we have two targets. The red objective is the first, which is as large as the size of the fence. The green goal compares to the size of the past up move, which ought to be applied beginning from the upper side of the hedge.

Bearish Pennant

As you have most likely speculated, the bearish hedge

is the equal representation of the bullish fence. Bearish hedges start with a value decline and end up with a balanced triangle appearance. Since hedges have pattern proceeding with character, bearish hedges are probably going to proceed with the bearish pattern.

At the point when the cost experiences the lower level of the bearish hedge, you should initially hope to catch the main objective, which is equivalent to the size of the fence itself. At the point when the value finishes this objective, you would then be able to attempt to get the further normal diminishing, which is equivalent to the size of the past leg or .618 of that leg. Allude to the picture underneath for a Bearish Pennant:

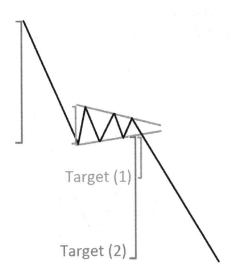

Expanding Triangle

You can scarcely ruin an extending triangle on the outline. The explanation behind this is it has one of a kind parameters. The two sides of the extending triangle are slanted, however, in inverse headings.

The course of the potential value move of this outline example is precarious to decide. In this way, we will currently present a couple of standards, which will assist you in identifying the heading of the average value moves.

Symmetrical Lines

And when the growing triangle is a flat, perfect representation of a balanced triangle, at that point, you should exchange the arrangement as a pattern continuation design. The picture beneath demonstrates a sketch of a growing triangle with stable lines:

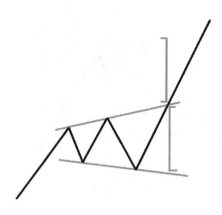

Increasing Lines

If the different sides of the ever-increasing triangle are expanding, at that point, the example is probably going to have bearish characters.

Decreasing Lines

If the different sides of the extending triangle arrangement are diminishing, at that point, the figure is probably going to have bullish potentials.

One Side Stronger than the Other One

If the highest points of the cost activity are expanding, yet the bottoms are diminishing with a higher force, at that point, the example has bearish character. Despite what might be expected, if the bases are decreasing, yet the tops are expanding with a higher force, at that point, the example is probably going to have bullish character. As it were, you should exchange the heading of the side, which has a higher tendency.

Trading: Triangles in Forex

Since we have examined the greater part of the significant triangle designs in Forex, I will presently demonstrate to you how a triangle exchanging framework could function.

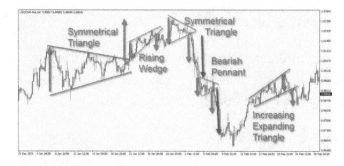

The picture above demonstrates the H4 diagram of the USD/CHF Forex pair for Jan – Feb 2016. The graph shows five triangle models and their likely results.

The diagram begins with a significant even triangle. The cost makes three diminishing tops and three expanding bottoms on the graph. The red bolt toward the start of the triangle estimates its size. As you see, a similar red flash is applied when the value breaks the upper degree of the triangle. The red glow demonstrates the potential objective of the example, which gets finished the following seven days.

Then, in transit up the value activity makes a rising wedge graph design. As we talked about, the rising wedge has bearish potential. With the breakout through the lower level of the wedge, we see a minor amendment. (yellow bolts)

Toward the finish of the bullish inclination, the value makes another balanced triangle. Later on, the amount gets through the lower level and finishes the size of the example (pink bolts).

While diminishing, the value activity makes a bearish hedge. This is the union after the primary motivation of the bearish pattern. The value breaks the lower level of the hedge subsequently. In transit down, we see the value finishing the main objective, which equivalents the size of the fence (red bolts). At that point, the lessening proceeds, and the decline is stretched out to a size equivalent to the last leg. (green pins).

The USD/CHF then makes a twofold base inversion example and changes to a bullish course. In transit up the value, activity makes a growing triangle design. Notice that both the lower and the upper level of the example are expanding. For this situation, the average value move is bearish and ought to be equivalent to the size of the case. Meanwhile, this time, the size of the matter is estimated from the closure side of the arrangement. The explanation behind this is we take the broadest side when we measure the standard move from the triangle breakout. The red bolts on the outline demonstrate to us that this example likewise finishes its objective.

Triangles are among the most significant diagram designs in Forex exchanging.

You have a contracting triangle on the outline when

the tops and the bottoms of the value activity are pushing toward one another.

The basic Forex triangles involve:

· Climbing Triangle: level tops, higher bottoms, bullish potential.

· Plummeting Triangle – level bottoms; lower lids; bearish potential;

· Wedges – sides increment/decline in a similar heading;

· Rising Wedge – higher tops; much higher bottoms; bearish potential;

· Falling Wedge – lower depths; even lower lids; bullish potential;

· Balanced Triangle – lower tops; higher bottoms; sides have a similar edge of development

· Bullish Pennant – comes after cost increment; closes with a little balanced triangle; bullish potential

· Bearish Pennant – comes after abatement; fastens with a bit of even triangle; bearish potential;

· Growing Triangle – sides move against one another. The capability of the growing triangle fluctuates relying upon the tendency of the line:

· Sides are Symmetrical – the potential value move is toward the pattern.

· The two Sides are Increasing – bearish likely

· The two Sides are Decreasing – bullish potential

CHAPTER 3

SWING TRADING BASICS: MEANING AND HOW IT WORKS

The way toward swing exchanging has turned into a well-known stock trading technique utilized by numerous dealers over the market. This style of exchanging has demonstrated to be exceptionally useful for some dedicated stocks and Forex dealers. Customarily swing exchanging has been characterized as a progressively theoretical methodology as the positions are generally purchased and held for the dealers foreordained time allotment. These time allotments could run somewhere in the range of two days to a couple of months. The objective of the swing broker is to distinguish the pattern either up or down and place their exchanges in the most invaluable position. From that point, the merchant will ride the design to what they decide as to the depletion point and sell for a benefit. Intermittently swing brokers will use a wide range of specialized markers that will enable them to have a progressively good likelihood when making their exchanges. Shorter-term brokers don't really will in general swing exchange as they lean toward holding positions for the day and practicing them preceding the end of the market. The swing exchanging technique uses time, and it is the time the impediment factor for long-time dealers. Generally, there is a lot of hazards associated with the end of the market and that a merchant won't acknowledge this hazard.

Swing exchanging is a style of exchanging that endeavors to catch increases a stock (or any monetary instrument) over a time of a couple of days to a little while. Swing brokers principally utilize specialized investigation to search for exchanging openings. These brokers may use principal examination, notwithstanding breaking down value patterns and examples.

Swing exchanging is a more extended term transferring style that expects persistence to hold your exchanges for a few days one after another. It is perfect for the individuals who can't screen their outlines for the day; however, they can devote two or three hours examining the market each night.

This is likely most appropriate for the individuals who have all day employments or school yet have enough extra time to keep awake-to-date with what is happening in the worldwide economies.

Swing exchanging endeavors to recognize "swings" inside a medium-term pattern and enter just when there is by all accounts a high likelihood of winning.

For instance, in an upturn, you intend to purchase (go long) at "swing lows." And on the other hand, sell (go short) at "swing highs" to exploit transitory countertrends.

Since exchanges last any longer than one day, more significant-stop misfortunes are to climate instability, and a forex merchant must adjust that to their cash the board plan.

You will, in all likelihood, observe exchanges conflict with you during the holding time since there can be numerous variances of the value during the shorter periods.

Significantly, you can try to avoid panicking during these occasions and trust in your examination.

Since exchanges more often than not have more significant targets, spreads won't have as quite a bit of an effect on your general benefits.

Thus, exchanging sets with bigger spreads, and lower liquidity is worthy.

You should be a swing dealer if:

You wouldn't fret holding your exchanges for a few days.

You are eager to take fewer exchanges; however, progressively cautious to ensure your transactions are generally excellent arrangements.

You wouldn't fret having enormous stop misfortunes.

You are understanding.

You can resist the urge to panic when exchanges move against you.

You might NOT have any desire to be a swing dealer if:

You like quick-paced, activity stuffed exchanging.

You are fretful and like to know whether you are correct or wrong right away.

You get sweat-soaked and on edge when exchanges conflict with you.

You can't put in two or three hours consistently to break down the business sectors.

You can't surrender your World of Warcraft striking sessions.

The differentiation of swing exchanging is an expansive point in that it has various impacts from a massive number of different exchanging procedures. These exchanging procedures are exciting and have their particular hazard profiles. Swing trading can be an excellent path for a market member to improve their specialized investigation abilities further while allowing them a chance to give more consideration to the leading site of the exchange. Numerous fruitful swing brokers have been known to utilize a Bollinger band procedure as an apparatus to help them in entering and leaving positions. For a swing dealer to be useful at the methodology, they should have a high bent for deciding the present market pattern and putting their situations as per that pattern. It makes a swing dealer note high to put a short position with the arrangement of holding for an all-inclusive timeframe in a market that is slanting upwards. The general subject here is that the objective of the dealers ought to be to build their likelihood of progress while restricting or wiping out hazard-totally. The swing dealer's most noticeably awful foe is that of a sideways or in a dynamic market. Sideways value activity will stop a swing merchant cold in their tracks as there is no overall pattern to key off.

At the point when utilized forcefully swing exchanging is a superb system used by numerous merchants crosswise over different markets. It isn't just in the Forex showcase; however, it is a critical apparatus in fates and value markets. Swing dealers take the abilities that they learn through specialized examination and can even parlay these aptitudes into different alternative techniques. The transient idea of swing exchanging separates it from that of the conventional speculator. Speculators will, in general, have a more extended term time skyline are not influenced by momentary value variances. As usual, one must recollect that swing exchanging is just a single technique and ought to be used only when adequately comprehended. Like any exchanging system, swing trading can be unsafe, and preservationist methodologies can transform into day exchanging procedures rapidly. When you utilize a swing exchanging system, guarantee that you completely comprehend the dangers and build up a technique that will have the option to enable you to produce the most significant rate returns on your positions.

Swing exchanging is one of transferring styles which generally executed in theoretical action in monetary markets, for example, securities, item, foreign trade, stock, and stock record. Usually, this exchanging style requires a swing dealer to hold their exchanging position more than one exchanging day, generally 2 to 5 exchanging days. Swing trading is mainstream in exchanging world as this transferring style, for the most part, has a decent hazard and reward proportion, it implies the likelihood to pick up benefit is higher than the risk that may ascend in each exchange.

By and large, swing exchanging goes for 100 pips benefit likelihood. Benefit potential can be picked up from each market swing. A swing broker, particularly in foreign trade and stock file advertise, can go both long or short of accepting each open door. It likewise implies, inside an exchanging week, when a market is unpredictable, a swing dealer may run over a few exchanging openings the individual in question can take.

Contrasted with scalping exchanging or day exchanging, clearly swing trading has less trading chances, notwithstanding, as should be visible here and whenever you execute this exchanging style, most likely you will have more opportunity to do your different exercises as you don't need to keep your eyes on a market all the exchanging day. You will get fewer chances, however, with a high likelihood of winning for every opportunity. It is your call to pick which exchanging style to apply. No exchanging style is immaculate, and there is always in addition to and short.

Presently, and when you surely need to give an attempt to swing exchanging, you can discover a few procedures from numerous assets accessible on the web. You may find a few books and some other instructive materials on swing exchanging. You can visit and be an individual from some exchanging discussions too. Notwithstanding, as regular, I need to advise you that there are likewise some shifty individuals guaranteeing themselves as swing exchanging masters; however, they need you to purchase their refuse training materials. Be mindful of such individuals.

Luckily, in the wake of getting some essential comprehension and experience on swing exchanging, you can be a decent swing merchant also. You can even think of your swing trading systems. Numerous individuals appreciate the advantage of building up their swing trading systems as they are the main ones who realize their exchanging character, need, and style. Never quit to figure out how to be a decent swing merchant, even though unquestionably, it will require some investment to ace swing exchanging brilliantly yet, at last, the majority of your endeavors will payout.

Issues With Swing Trading Using Options

Swing exchanging is one of the most widely recognized methods for trading the securities exchange. Regardless of whether you know it or not, you presumably have been swing exchanging all these while. Swing trading is purchasing every so often selling a couple of days or weeks after the fact when costs are higher, or lower (on account of a short). Such a cost increment or lessening is known as a "Value Swing," subsequently the expression "Swing Trading."

Most learners to choices exchanging take up opportunities as a type of influence for their swing exchanging. They need to purchase call choices when costs are low and afterward rapidly sell them a couple of days or weeks after the fact for a utilized addition. The other way around valid for put choices. In any case, many such amateurs immediately discovered the most painful way possible that in options swing exchanging, and they could, in any case, make a generous misfortune regardless of whether the stock inevitably moved toward the path that they anticipated.

How is that so? What are a few issues related to swing exchanging utilizing alternatives that they neglected to observe?

For sure, although choices can be utilized just as utilized substitution for exchanging the underlying stock, there are a couple of things about alternatives that most tenderfoots neglect to observe.

1) Strike Price

It doesn't take long for anybody to understand that there are numerous alternatives accessible crosswise over many strike costs for every single optionable stock. The undeniable decision that fledglings generally make is to purchase the "modest" out of the cash alternatives for more significant influence. Out of the cash, choices are alternatives that have no work in an incentive in them. These are called options with strike costs higher than the overarching stock cost or put choices with strike costs lower than the overall stock cost.

The issue with purchasing out of the cash alternatives in swing exchanging is that regardless of whether the essential stock move toward your expectation (upwards for purchasing call choices and downwards for purchasing put choices), you could at present lose ALL your cash if the stock didn't surpass the strike cost of the options you bought! The truth is out; this is known as to "Lapse Out Of The Money" which makes every one of the choices you purchased useless. This is likewise how most fledglings lose all their cash in choices exchanging.

By and large, the more out of the cash the choices are, the higher the influence, and the higher the hazard that those alternatives will terminate useless, losing all of you the capital put into them. The more in cash the choices are, the lower increasingly costly they are because of the worth incorporated with them; the lower the influence turns out to be, nevertheless, the more economical the danger of terminating useless. You have to take the average extent of the move and the measure of hazard you can mull over when choosing which strike cost to purchase for swing exchanging with choices. And when you anticipate a significant move, out of the cash choices would give you immense rewards, yet if the movie neglects to surpass the strike cost of those choices by termination, a terrible arousing is standing by.

2) Expiration Date

Not at all like swing exchanging with stocks which you can clutch never-ending when things turn out badly, have alternatives of a distinct lapse date. It means that you are incorrect; you will rapidly lose cash when lapse lands without the advantage of having the option to clutch the position and hang tight for arrival or profit.

Indeed, swing exchanging with choices is battling against time. The quicker the stock moves, the surer you are of benefit. The uplifting news is, all optional stocks have options crosswise over numerous termination months too. Closer month options are less expensive, and further month alternatives are progressively costly. All things considered, when you are sure that the hidden stock is going to hurry, you could exchange with closer termination month alternatives or what we call "Front Month Options," which are less expensive and subsequently have a more significant influence.

Exchange forex and CFDs on stock files, products, stocks, metals, and energies are with an authorized and controlled representative. For all customers who open their first genuine record, XM offers up to $5000 store reward to test the XM items and administrations with no underlying store required. Study how you can exchange more than 1000 instruments on the XM MT4 and MT5 stages from your PC and Mac, or an assortment of cell phones.

The amount Money Do I Need to Swing Trade Stocks?

Keen on swing exchanging stocks–taking exchanges that last a couple of days to half a month and thinking about what amount of cash you have to begin? How much capital you'll need is reliant on the procedure you use, which at that point influences the amount you chance per exchange and your position size.

Markets You Can Swing Trade

Swing exchanging is taking a place that could take the most recent days to half a month (possibly several months for individual brokers/exchanges). To what extent a swing exchange keeps going relies upon the procedure you're utilizing and what you anticipate from your trades. And when a stock moves typically 1% every day, and it needs to move 10% so as to arrive at your objective (where you need to get out with a benefit), it could take half a month or more before the value advances toward your leave point (if current conditions proceed).

Swing brokers hold positions medium-term, in contrast to informal investors (perceive How Much Money Do I Need to Become a Day Trader?) who close all situations before the day closes. Procedures shift by swing dealer. However, the first spotlight is on force swing merchants need to catch a conventional piece of value development in the most limited measure of time conceivable. At the point when the value energy closes, swing brokers proceed onward to different chances.

This style of exchanging should be possible in many markets (stocks, forex, fates and choices, for instance), which have the development you can benefit from (profit!). Swing exchanging stocks is well known because there's continuously a stock moving with force someplace.

Forex is likewise mainstream because, for the most part, there's a money pair (or a few) that are moving admirably. Prospects are also exceptionally mainstream among day and swing merchants, offering a full cluster of items (for example, gold, bonds, stock records, instability, espresso, and so forth) to exchange. Swing exchanging forex requires less capital than stock and is hence a decent choice And when you need more cash-flow to swing exchange stocks.

Take a look at specific situations in the financial exchange, so you can perceive how a lot of cash you'll have to turn into a securities exchange swing merchant.

Issue of Under-Capitalization When Swing Trading Stocks

Having more capital in your record is superior to less. One primary slip-up dealers are under-promoted. In the stock, advertise being under-promoted can without much of a stretch occur particularly to new brokers if their record drops in worth.

As showed, to make it worth our time and energy, we ought to change in any event $100 per exchange. Along these lines, our victors won't be disintegrated by commissions and expenses. Be that as it may, And when we hazard $100, what occurs if a dealer's record parity drops to $4,000? Presently they are gambling 2.5% on each exchange. If things still don't go well, and the equality drops to $3,000, the broker is currently risking 3.3% per trade they are risking more as their presentation deteriorates!

If your record parity dips under $5,000, STOP TRADING, since you can never again bear to lose $100 and still keep the record hazard to under 2%. Likewise, And when you opened a record with $15,000, and you said you would hazard 1% exchange, if your parity falls beneath $10,000, quit exchanging. And when you continue trading with an equalization beneath $10,000, you will hazard over 1% (gambling at any rate $100 per exchange).

Top up your record to bring it back above $5,000 (or $10,000 if gambling 1%) And whenever you are as yet particular about your technique (or are eager to place in an opportunity to make it work), or just pick not to exchange until you are in a superior situation to do as such.

Cash Needed to Swing Trade Stocks – Final Word

The snappiest method to perceive how a lot of capital you need is to utilize the pursued equation:

Exchange chance x position size x (100%/account hazard %) = Capital Required.

Expect your chance 1% of your record, purchase 100 offers, and your exchange hazard is $2 (purchase at

$38 and stop misfortune at $36). Module the numbers:

$2 x 100 x 100 = $20,000. That is the amount you have to make that exchange. You could use influence (up to 2:1), which implies that you need $10K in the record to make this because with influence, you will have the required $20K. You will need to have more in the record than the definite sum you need!

In case you're willing to chance 2% of your record per exchange:

$2 x 100 x 50 = $10,000 capital required.

Record hazards and exchange hazards help you decide how much capital you will require. Each exchange is somewhat unique, with various exchange dangers and position sizes. Record for that when determining the amount you will store. Concentrate the stock graphs, choose how and where you will enter and where you will put a stop misfortune.

When in doubt, you will require at any rate $5,000 to $10,000 to swing exchange stocks successfully. It is prescribed you store more than the base, supposing that you save the absolute minimum a couple losing exchanges will put you beneath the suggestion record balance.

It's smarter to hold up a couple of months and set aside more capital than to surge in under-promoted and likely lose everything. Utilize an opportunity to rehearse while you set aside!

Swing Trading - How to Trade?

Key learning:

It sounds incredible when you consider swing stock exchange; however, the majority of the brokers are unconscious of the technique on the best way to exchange. In swing, transferring the merchant by and large revels into buying the stocks toward the path where the pattern is stable. In straightforward words, the swing merchant will never exchange the course, which isn't in the stream and not coordinating up the design. These exchanges are hung on for a couple of days, and as a rule, they monitor the higher time allotment outlines, which are around 1 hour and more than that while you are observing and setting your exchanges.

There are a few recognized manners by which a swing dealer can without much of a stretch spot his/her exchanges and that additionally toward the prevalent pattern. The standard and effective practice are to sit tight at the cost level to remake previously, and you have to enter your exchange before it reaches out towards on stream. The passage is done for the most part based on value resounding off of help or opposition levels, pattern lines, or by and large it might require marker check.

In swing stock exchanging, the swing financial specialists or brokers can without much of a stretch have the chances heaped in their benefit by watching the more prominent and more significant period graphs and by entering the exchanges just the method for meaningful patterns in the securities exchange. These will make your business an incredible style of exchanging regardless of the securities exchange.

Figure out How to Swing Trade: In request to figure out how to swing exchange, you have to have the authority over the central segments of the exchanging. Every one of the subtleties that are talked about underneath structures the structure hinders the swing stock trading and are the reasons why outrageous expert financial specialists are incredibly beneficial.

This territory grasps the accompanying:

o Trading brain science -

You have to create adjusted Psychology to wind up fit for exchanging effectively.

o The money, the executives -

This administration allows a merchant to limit the dangers and to expand the arrival esteem on their rewards.

o Market investigation -

In the assessment, there are two different ways, which are Technical and essential investigation.

o Japanese candle graphs -

It is the main component to have an inside investigation of the financial exchange and its feelings. You should be for perusing and understanding the Japanese candle arrangements.

o Trend Identification -

The swing brokers increment their chances by exchanging the course of the pattern. You have to discover the right design.

o Support and opposition levels -

These two levels grant the merchant to locate the pivotal degrees of the securities exchange where the patterns are in the dealer's support.

o Fibonacci retracement levels -

Much the same as the help and obstruction levels, the Fibonacci retracement levels additionally enable you to have a decent passage into the market.

o Trading markers -

The apprentices must take a gander at the pointers, which are commonly utilized by the banks and expert financial specialists in swing exchanging.

o Stop misfortune -

Stop misfortunes bring about only a little harm; accordingly, it's disregarded by the majority of the newcomers around here.

o Trading hours -

Continuously cause a decent search and after that to find your hours that are appropriate for the opening and shutting of the trades.

Swing Trading: Swing Trading Stock That Help You Earn More

The term alludes to the different styles of swing exchanging stock, items, or list. This exchanging is an exchanging practice where the merchant purchases or sells the instrument at or close to the finish of a down or up value swing in the ware. This swing is caused either because of day by day value unpredictability or week by week value instability. Information on these styles encourages him to become a beneficial dealer and puts him on the way of effectual exchanging calling.

The time furthest reaches that is typically associated with holding the instrument by the merchant is 1-4 days. It is, for the most part, not precisely seven days, regardless. The money or the swing is exchanging stock, which the merchant is managing in swings starting with one value level then onto the next. A swing broker rides on this wavering or swing that the market makes on the stock. That implies he purchases the instruments toward market patterns, and he doesn't exchange by conflicting with the significant trends in the market.

There are various manners by which he can put an exchange. The most well-known method for doing it toward market pattern is to sit tight at the costs swing, exchanging stock to return or backtrack and afterward enter an exchange before it goes onwards. It is the most secure technique as he can stack the chances in support of him by watching the higher period graphs, and after that enters the exchange, the bearing of significant pattern likewise got back to the draw time. There are some essential components of swing exchanging that should be aced to turn into a capable dealer.

The above all else component in learning the swing exchanging business is a comprehension of the exchanging brain research. The other significant viewpoint requires knowledge of the meaningful patterns of the market. It causes him to distinguish the model effectively in the market and increase from it. The third considerable viewpoint is the dealer's capacity to oversee cash with the goal that he container expand gains and limit dangers. The dealer ought to likewise have the option to peruse and comprehend the Japanese Candlestick development to get a vibe of the market opinions. Another component that is urgent to his prosperity is to have the option to discover the best exchanging hours to open and close the exchange.

Different fundamentals of a decent merchant are to find what pointers are utilized by other expert dealers to run swing exchanging effectively. He should likewise be knowledgeable about the Trading markers used by different banks. He ought to also have the option to distinguish the specialized market investigation and the essential market examination as the two most significant styles to break down the market. Among another component of the swing exchanging business is the information of help and obstruction levels, Fibonacci retracement level, stop misfortune, and recognizable proof of pattern lines.

The dealer needs to acclimate himself with this data to begin his voyage to turning into an effective swing broker.

Swing Trading Stocks - An Insight to Pros and Cons

There are sure contrasts between Swing Trading Stocks and Day Trading. Day Trading is identified with a specific timeframe, though Swing exchanging likewise delineates a specific timeframe. Swing exchanging includes a timespan that is longer than the staring off into space-time range and shorter than somebody who is headed to contribute and exchange for a more extended timeframe. If there should be an occurrence of records and assessment purposes, whatever is not exactly a year is imagined as a transient exchanging the financial exchange, and anything that is about a multi-year or more is considered as long haul evaluating.

Swing exchanging is a novel style of exchanging and venture. It is reasonable for each one of the individuals who need to exchange for a more extended timeframe than a day trading and have a decent learning of swing transferring procedures. The informal investors enter and exit around the same time and in a similar position. The swing merchants would leave their exchange of stocks and items to be open for a couple of weeks, which can stretch out as long as a couple of months. The merchants work as indicated by the swing exchanging methodologies they know.

Swing Trading Stocks Pros and Cons:

Like all other things, Swing exchanging has its high side and awful side. Bothe the day trading and swing trading are similarly dangerous, which relies upon the experience, specialized assessment and brain science as upheld by the merchant. Continuously recollect the standard that is, the more drawn out the time of exchange the market, the higher the hazard factor.

The Pros of Swing Trading Stocks-

*It is less tedious than the day exchanging segment.

*A dealer possesses more energy for the assessment of the best-exchanging methods between the exchanges, and like this, the broker can most likely choose great and fascinating entertainers.

*The first section which is reduced is offered time to get recuperated from the harm and afterward go to a positive level or state-contingent upon the bearing the merchant has chosen. It is said that a long position that is upward posts are substantially more superior to the principal short area that is descending location.

*Swing Traders doesn't require to address the issues of the 'Example Day Trader.'

*Swing merchants are permitted to have more information for concentrate as indicated by the period than the informal investors.

*A swing broker is progressively sure and certain about his/her exchange because the ongoing pattern of exchanging is bolstered by the long haul information from the history.

The Cons of Swing Trading Stocks-

*Definitely the swing trader consumes less time and possesses more energy for the assessment of the best-exchanging methods between the exchanges and accordingly, the dealer can likely choose great and fascinating entertainers.

The con: is that a swing merchant may get awful information and subtleties into the information assessment and might choose a less valuable stock execution or lost stock or item.

*The first passage which is weak is offered time to get recuperated from the harm and after that go to a positive level or state-contingent upon the heading, the broker has chosen. It is suggested that a long position that is upward posts are substantially more superior to the primary short area that is descending location.

The Con: the main miserable and awful section has the opportunity to get going the other way to the trade.

CHAPTER 4

STOCK MARKET:

Newbie financial exchange speculators are the individuals who have moderately simple learning and involvement in the contributing circle. The more significant part of these people, for the most part, start by adhering to a 'purchase and hold' exchanging methodology. As a tenderfoot, your extensive involvement in financial exchange ventures in trading. Generally, it limits you to making close to a few exchanges maybe on a month to month premise from a money account. In any case, this doesn't essential connote that you have not set high requirements on your financial exchange exchanging exercises. You, in all likelihood, are keen on extending your insight just as speculation involvement in understanding the goals you may have set. It is all pleasant and great.

As a rule, it is continuously extreme for youngsters to observe timberland from just trees. Additionally, they think that it's difficult to perceive if the future possibilities of a specific security are favorable, regardless of whether the momentary exchanging patterns are not unpredictable. Apprentices are regularly competent during robust 'buyer' markets. Be that as it may, shockingly get themselves confused on harder events, mainly when market unpredictability is higher, and 'bears' happen to run the show. Ithe event that you profoundly feel you fit this depiction to the T, here then are some financial exchange venture nuts and bolts for learners, which could be helpful.

Mistakes you should consider

#1 Not Understanding the Investment in question

One of the world's best financial specialists, Warren Buffett, alerts against putting resources into organizations you don't get it. This implies you try not to purchase stock in organizations when you don't comprehend the plans of action.

#2 Falling in Love With a Company in particular

Time after time, when we see an organization we've put resources into progress nicely, it's anything but difficult to experience passionate feelings for it and overlook that we purchased the stock as a venture.

#3 Lack of Patience

How often has the intensity of gradual advancement turned out to be unavoidably clear? Gradual more often than not beats the competition - be it at the exercise center, in school, or your vocation. Why, at that point, do we anticipate that it should be unique about contributing? A moderate, consistent, and taught approach would go significantly further as time goes on than going for the latest possible time.

#4 Too Much Investment Turnover

Turnover, or hopping all through positions, is another arrival executioner. Except if you're an institutional financial specialist with the advantage of low commission rates, the exchange expenses can destroy you - also the momentary assessment rates and the open door cost of passing up the long haul increases of wise speculations.

It is crucial for you to completely comprehend that all individuals have to change degrees of hazard resilience. It surely implies there is nothing of the sort as 'right equalization' in this given issue.

It typically prompts a diminishing of the general nervousness you will undoubtedly encounter when you exchange or put resources into the securities exchange, due to your 'view' of the dangers in question. In this way, by setting aside the vital effort to completely comprehend your accurate hazard resistance, you will have the option to abstain from exchanging ventures you fear. In a perfect world, you ought not to put resources into an advantage, which can cause you restless evenings. Tension triggers dread that, in its turn, prompts a passionate reaction to the stressor. By continually holding a calm mind during securities exchange vulnerability, you will have the option to cling to an 'apathetic' necessary leadership process in your financial exchange exercises.

Make it a propensity to keep off your feelings from your ventures.

By a wide margin, the most significant obstruction a seriously huge number of amateurs need to face routinely is their failure to direct their feelings and continue to settle on sensible choices. For the time being, the costs of organization stocks relate to the consolidated feelings of the entire venture network. At the point when most securities exchange financial specialists happen to be on edge about a specific firm, it's stock costs will undoubtedly dive in. On the other hand, when most dealers have a positive point of view to a firm, it's stock costs will generally rise.

Those people who hold a pessimistic point of view about the securities exchange are known as 'bears.' While those that have inspirational standpoints to the equivalent are known as 'bulls.' During market hours, the persistent battle among bulls and bears thought about the continually fluctuating protections' costs. These transient changes by and large emerge from bits of gossip, hypotheses, and at times even expectation. These components can be marked as being feelings. A successful financial exchange venture requires a legitimate and efficient investigation of an organization's benefits, the board, and future possibilities.

Managing all these puzzling considerations can trigger a great deal of stress, especially and when you always screen the costs of the protections you exchange. This feeling can, in the end, brief, you take certain activities. As your feelings are the primary inspiration, it is for the most part, and likely your business will not be right. At the point when you purchase a stock, you should do as such for legitimate reasons. Likewise, you ought to have practical desires for precisely how the costs will perform if your controlling rights demonstrate to be exact. At long last, before putting resources into any stock, consistently set aside an effort to decide the definite point you will sell your property, particularly if your reasons are refuted. With everything taken into account, always have a suitable 'leave' system before buying any stock, and make it a point to execute it apathetically.

Make it your business to extensively find out about the nuts and bolts of financial exchange speculation.

Preceding making your absolute first financial

exchange venture or exchange, ensure that you see entirely every one of the nuts and bolts of the economic transaction together with the individual protections which make them up. The following are the absolute most appropriate zones you will be obliged to be well familiar with before starting any securities exchange exercises.

Make it a point to expand your securities exchange ventures.

The minute you have played out all the vital research that encourages you to decide and even measure chance, settling on the choice to differentiate your financial exchange portfolio can be an extremely wise advance. The equivalent is additionally the situation when you are absolutely 'agreeable' that you will have the option to pinpoint any potential threat, which may gently imperil your case. In the two locations, you will have the opportunity to sell your securities exchange speculations preceding continuing any risky misfortune.

The essential main thrust which persuades them to do so is the firm assurance that a separate ominous occasion can never impact every one of their property. What this truly comes down to is the evident certainty that stock expansion can permit to quickly recuperate from the departure of a solitary and even a few of your speculations.

The most common errors not to commit

Securities exchange contributing is a dangerous game, specific if you are an unpracticed financial specialist. And when you are not cautious, you can undoubtedly observe your capital dissolve rapidly.

1. Putting resources into little top organizations.

I have been purchasing and selling shares for quite a long while now. However, regardless, it astounds me that such vast numbers of novice financial specialists toss the majority of their money into little top organizations searching for the following five-bagger or ten-bagger. They will peruse different securities exchange gatherings. They will be urged to become tied up with these modest organizations that are tipped to be the following enormous thing, yet a large portion of them will, at last, come up short, so it's mostly only betting.

A much-improved methodology is to adhere to the reliably productive huge top organizations at first, and ideally, those that have a long record of conveying development in both income and profits. At that point, you are experienced, you could then begin pondering enhancing your portfolio to incorporate a little level of little top organizations also if you so wish. There's nothing amiss with having a couple of high-chance interests in your wallet as long as the remainder of your collection comprises of increasingly secure ventures.

2. Having an uneven portfolio.

This pursues on from the last point in that you should never overextend yourself far. At the end of the day, you ought to never put all your cash into only a couple of organizations, and you should attempt to put your money crosswise over organizations in various areas if you can to spread your hazard. Inability to do so may leave you overexposed, and it could disastrously affect your portfolio if the area you are put resources into, or the bunch of organizations you are put resources into, goes down.

3. Putting resources into shares without utilizing a stop misfortune.

One of the most widely recognized errors made by unpracticed financial specialists is that they tenaciously won't utilize a stop misfortune. Presently there might be contention for saying that you needn't bother with a stop misfortune and when you are contributing Warren Buffet-style with a ten or multi-year standpoint; however, as a rule, you should adhere to a stop misfortune to contain your troubles.

See Northern Rock or any of the other UK banks, for example. If you had put resources into these organizations a year or two back, you would have seen your ventures decreased to virtually nothing. Yet, And when you had utilized a stop loss of state 10% or 20%, at that point, you would have been consequently halted out quite a while prior, and the more significant part of your capital would now be flawless.

The primary most normal slip-up I see financial specialists make is purchasing stocks basically because they are modest. There is nothing of the sort as a small stock dependent on the value alone. And when a stock cost is 50 dollars, and it controls one thousand dollars worth of advantages, then that is a great arrangement, however, it isn't as great of a method if another stock was 100 dollars and the 100 dollar stock controlled 10 thousand dollars in resources. The model could never occur, all things considered; however, the fact of the matter is essentially asking yourself what amount genuine worth am I purchasing when I put resources into this organization?

The following most significant errors speculators make is relating an organization to individual reasoning and issues that are not founded on monetary sense and expectation by any stretch of the imagination. Some of the time, individuals put resources into organizations basically because they like the organization by and by. Nothing could be an awful thought than to put resources into an organization dependent on the sheer actuality that you by and by like it. Other individuals could like the organization you want, and the organization, the executives, might be ghastly. A few people additionally contribute dependent on senseless diagram examples and volume, which infrequently work when they are utilized, putting resources into the securities exchange. Warren Buffet and numerous different renowned speculators have expressed that seeing graph examples and volume prompts disarray and seldom benefit. The facts confirm that a few brokers have made cash off specialized diagram designs, yet what a number of them reliably profit, and what the name of wealthy transient dealers do you know?

If we can work around all the mental impedances that keep us down when we purchase organizations, we CAN profit for a more secure, more joyful future over the long haul. It's every one of them a fundamental matter of purchasing all-around run great organizations, and after that clutching them for their future monetary worth

The speculation scene can be compelling and regularly advancing. In any case, the individuals who set aside the effort to comprehend the essential standards and the diverse resource classes remain to pick up altogether as time goes on. The initial step: figuring out how to recognize various kinds of ventures and what rung each involves on the "hazard stepping stool."

Nugget

Contributing can be an overwhelming possibility for apprentices, with a massive assortment of potential advantages for add to a portfolio.

The venture 'hazard stepping stool' recognizes resource classes dependent on their relative peril, with money being the most steady and elective speculations regularly being the most unstable.

Staying with list assets or trade exchanged finances that mirror the market is frequently the best way for another financial specialist.

Understanding the Investment 'Hazard Ladder'

Here are the significant resource classes, in a rising request of hazard, on the venture hazard stepping stool.

Money

A money bank store is the least difficult, most effectively reasonable venture resource—and the most secure. In addition to the fact that it gives financial specialists exact information about the premium, they'll acquire. However, it additionally ensures they'll recover their capital. On the drawback, the premium earned from money stored in a bank account only here and there beats expansion. Declarations of Deposit (CDs) are profoundly fluid instruments, fundamentally the same as money that are instruments that usually give higher loan fees than those in bank accounts. Be that as it may, cash is bolted up for a while, and there are potential early withdrawal punishments included.

Bonds

A bond is an obligation instrument speaking to an advance made by a speculator to a borrower. A run of the mill security will include either a partnership or an administration organization, where the borrower will give a fixed financing cost to the moneylender in return for utilizing their capital. Bonds are typical in associations that utilization them to back tasks, buys, or different undertakings.

The loan costs dictate security rates. Because of this, they are exchanged during times of quantitative facilitating or when the Federal Reserve—or other national banks—raise financing costs.

Stocks

Portions of stock let financial specialists take an interest in the organization's prosperity utilizing increments in the stock's cost and through profits.

Investors have a case on the organization's benefits in case of liquidation (that is, the organization failing); however, they don't possess the advantages. Holders of regular stock appreciate casting ballot rights at investors' gatherings. Holders of favored stock don't have casting ballot rights yet get inclination over ordinary investors as far as the profit installments.

Common Funds

A natural reserve is a kind of speculation where more than one speculator pools their cash together to buy protections. Shared assets are not detached, as they are overseen by portfolio directors who designate and circulate the pooled venture into stocks, bonds, and different protections. People may put resources into shared assets for as little as $1,000/share, giving them a chance to differentiate into upwards of 100 individual stocks contained inside a given portfolio.

Shared assets are, in some cases, intended to emulate hidden lists, for example, the S&P 500 or DOW Industrial Index. There are likewise numerous common supports that are seen, which means they are refreshed by portfolio directors who cautiously track and modify their assignments inside the reserve. Nonetheless, these assets, by and large, have more prominent costs, for example, yearly administration expenses and front-end charges—which can cut into a financial specialist's profits.

Shared assets are esteemed toward the finish of the exchanging day, and all purchase and sale exchanges are in like manner executed after the market closes.

Exchange-Traded Funds (ETFs)

Exchange-Traded Funds (ETFs) have turned out to be very prevalent since their presentation back in the mid-1990s. ETFs are like common assets. However, they exchange for the day on a stock trade. Along these lines, they reflect the purchase and-sell conduct of stocks. This likewise implies their worth can change radically over an exchanging day.

ETFs can follow a hidden file, for example, the S&P 500 or some other "bushel" of stocks the backer of the ETF needs to underline a particular ETF with. It can incorporate anything from developing markets, items, singular business areas, for example, biotechnology or agribusiness, and the sky is the limit from there. Because of the simplicity of exchanging and broad inclusion, ETFs are well known for financial specialists.

The most common errors not to commit in ETFs

1. Being Late

Maybe the most significant slip-up with supporting is that most races to do it sometime later. That is, speculators, scramble to ensure their portfolios directly after their positions have begun to cause soak misfortunes. When a market pullback has started, you can hope to pay a higher premium for security in the choices advertise, which is the place many will go to.

2. Not Hedging for the Right Exposure

Another typical oversight with regards to supporting with ETFs is identified with financial specialists not building a particular enough arrangement, mainly on account of securing against occasion hazard. One slip-up to maintain a strategic distance from is jumbling your exposures.

For instance, if you need to fence your value portfolio comprising fundamentally of little tops, make sure to choose the proper instrument; for example, picking a backward Russell 2000 ETF over an S&P 500 one.

The other absence of particularity is increasingly quantitative.

3. Over-Hedging

There is plenty of proof that supports long haul contributing. So in case, you're a long haul financial specialist, attempting to shield your portfolio from each adjustment or occasion hazard is a surefire approach to pay a high premium for the protection you never indeed plan to utilize. Put another way, and you may accomplish more damage to your portfolio if you attempt to effectively ensure it as opposed to leaving it be (make a point to expand and rebalance).

Understandable and necessary, you most likely don't have to support for occasion hazard except if you wish to be exceptionally strategic.

Elective Investments

There is an immense universe of elective speculations, including the accompanying parts:

Land. Financial specialists can secure areas by legitimately purchasing a business or private property. On the other hand, they can partake in land speculation trusts (REITs). REITs act like common assets wherein a gathering of speculators pool their cash together to buy properties. They exchange like stocks on a similar trade.

Flexible investments and private value reserves. Flexible investments, which may put resources into a range of benefits intended to convey past market returns, called "alpha." However, execution isn't ensured, and mutual funds can see fantastic moves in yields, here and there failing to meet expectations the market by a noteworthy edge. Commonly just accessible to authorize financial specialists, these vehicles regularly require high introductory speculations of $1 at least million. They likewise will, in general, force total assets prerequisites. Both venture types may tie up a financial specialist's cash for significant timespans.

Products. Items allude to substantial assets, for example, gold, silver, raw petroleum, just as rural items.

The most effective method to Invest Sensibly, Suitably and Simply

Numerous veteran speculators expand their portfolios utilizing the benefit classes recorded above, with the blend mirroring their resilience for hazard. An excellent recommendation to financial specialists is, to begin with, essential ventures, at that point, gradually extend their portfolios. In particular, shared assets or ETF's trade exchanged assets are a decent initial step before proceeding onward to individual stocks, land, and other elective ventures.

In any case, the vast majority are too occupied to even think about worrying about observing their portfolios every day. In this manner, staying with list subsidizes that mirror the market is a practical arrangement. Steven Goldberg, ahead at the firm Tweddell Goldberg Investment Management and long-term shared finances writer at Kiplinger.com, further contends that most people need three list reserves: one covering the U.S. value advertise, another with global benefits and the third following a bond file.

CHAPTER 5

OPTIONS TRADING:

What are the options?

An option is an agreement that permits (yet doesn't require) a financial specialist to purchase or sell a hidden instrument like a security, ETF, or even list at a foreordained cost over a specific timeframe. Buying and selling options are done on the alternatives advertise, which exchanges agreements dependent on protections. Purchasing an alternative that enables you to buy shares sometime in the future is known as a "call options," though buying an option that allows you to sell shares sometime in the not too distant future is known as a "put options."

Nonetheless, options are not a similar thing as stocks since they don't speak to proprietorship in an organization. What's more, even though fates use contracts simply as options do, alternatives viewed as a lower hazard because of the way that you can pull back (or leave) An option contract anytime. The cost of the options (it's premium) is, therefore, a level of the hidden resource or security.

114

When purchasing or selling alternatives, the speculator or merchant has the option to practice those options anytime up until the lapse date - so essentially buying or selling an opportunity doesn't mean you need to practice it at the purchase/sell point. In light of this framework, alternatives viewed as subsidiary protections - which means their cost gotten from something different (for this situation, from the estimation of advantages like the market, protections, or other hidden instruments). Hence, alternatives viewed as less unsafe than stocks (whenever utilized effectively).

Be that as it may, for what reason would financial specialist use options? Purchasing options are fundamentally wagering on stocks to go up, down, or to support an exchanging Position the market.

The cost at which you consent to purchase the underlying security using the options is known as the "strike cost," and the charge you pay for buying that alternative agreement is known as the "superior." When deciding the strike value, you are wagering that the benefit (regularly a stock) will go up or down in cost. The amount you are paying for that wagered is superior, which is a level of the estimation of that advantage.

There are two various types of options - call and put options - which give the speculator the right (however not commitment) to sell or purchase protections.

Call Options

A call option is an agreement that gives the financial specialist the privilege to purchase a specific measure of offers (regularly 100 for every transaction) of a particular security or item at a predefined cost over a particular test of time. For instance, call options would enable a dealer to purchase a specific action of portions of either stock, bonds, or even different instruments like ETFs or lists at a later time (by the termination of the agreement).

In case you're purchasing a call option, it implies you need the stock (or other security) to go up in cost with the goal that you can make a benefit off of your agreement by practicing your entitlement to purchase those stocks (and usually quickly offer them to capitalize on the advantage).

The expense you are paying to purchase the call options is known as the top-notch (it's the expense of buying the agreement which will enable you to in the end buy the stock or security). In this sense, the premium of the call alternative is similar to an upfront installment like you would put on a house or vehicle. When buying a call, alternatively, you concur with the dealer on a strike cost. You are given the option to purchase the security at a foreordained value (which doesn't change until the agreement terminates).

Be that as it may, for what reason would a financial specialist use alternatives? Purchasing options are fundamentally wagering on stocks to go up, down, or to support an exchanging position in the market.

The cost at which you consent to purchase the fundamental security utilizing the alternative is known as the "strike cost," and the expense you pay for purchasing that options agreement is known as the "superior." When deciding the strike value, you are wagering that the advantage (ordinarily a stock) will go up or down in cost. The amount you are paying for that wagered is top-notch, which is a level of the estimation of that benefit.

There are two various types of options - call and put alternatives - which give the financial specialist the right (yet not commitment) to sell or purchase protections.

Thus, call alternatives are additionally a lot of same protection - you are paying for an agreement that terminates at a set time yet enables you to buy a security (like a stock) at a foreordained value (which won't go up regardless of whether the cost of the inventory available does). In any case, you should reestablish your options (commonly on week after week, month to month, or quarterly premise). Thus, alternatives are continually encountering what's called time rot - which means their worth decompositions after some time.

For call options, the lower the strike value, the more inherent worth the call alternative has.

Put Options

On the other hand, a put alternative is an agreement that gives the speculator the privilege to sell a specific measure of offers (once more, regularly 100 for each transaction) of a particular security or ware at a predefined cost over a particular standard of time. Much the same as call options, a put option permits the broker the right (however not commitment) to sell a security by the agreement's termination date.

Much the same as call options, the cost at which you consent to sell the stock is known as the strike cost, and the premium is the expense you are paying for the put alternative.

Put options work likewise to calls, except you need the security to drop in cost if you are purchasing taken care of alternative to make a benefit (or sell the put options and when you figure the price will go up).

On the in spite of call options, with put alternatives, the higher the strike value, the more intrinsic worth the put options have.

Long versus Short Options

Not at all like different protections like fates contracts,

are alternatives exchanging commonly a "long" - which means you are purchasing the options with the expectations of the value going up (in which case you would buy call options). In any case, regardless of whether you purchase put options (appropriate to sell the security), you are as yet purchasing extended options.

Shorting an option is selling that alternative. However, the benefits of the deal are constrained to the premium of the opportunities - and, the hazard is boundless.

For both call and put options, the additional time left on the agreement, the higher the premiums will be.

It is frequently that a few people discover the Option's idea hard to see; however, they have just tailed it in their different exchanges, for example, vehicle protection or home loans. In this part, it is impudent to know the absolute most significant parts of Options exchanging before we get down to the universe of alternatives trading.

Options terminologies

Strike Price

The Strike Price is the cost at which the underlying stocks can be purchased or sold according to the agreement. In options exchanging, the Strike Price for a Call Option demonstrates the value at which the

Stock can be bought (at the very latest its lapse) and for Put Options exchanging it alludes to the cost at which the dealer can practice its entitlement to sell the hidden stocks (before its termination)

Premium

Since the Options themselves don't have an essential worth, the Options premium is the value that you need to pay to buy an option. The bonus is controlled by different components, including the hidden stock value, unpredictability in the market, and the days until the Option's termination. In alternatives exchanging, picking the premium is one of the most significant segments.

Fundamental Asset

In alternatives exchanging, the essential resource can be stocks, fates, records, item, or money. The cost of Options gotten from its structural support. The Option of capital gives the privilege to purchase or sell the stock at a particular cost and date to the holder — subsequently, it is about the hidden resource or stocks with regards to Stock in Options Trading.

Lapse Date

In options exchanging, every investment opportunity has a termination date. The termination date is additionally the keep going date on which the Options holder can practice the privilege to purchase or sell the Options that are in holding. In Options Trading, the termination of Options can shift from weeks to months to year's contingent available and the guidelines.

Alternatives Style

There are two significant sorts of Options that are drilled in the vast majority of the alternatives exchanging markets.

(ITM, OTM and ATM)

It is essential to comprehend the Options before you start exchanging Stock Options. A lot of alternatives exchanging methodologies are played around the option.

It essentially characterizes the connection between the strike cost of an option and the present value of the underlying Stocks. We will analyze each term in detail beneath.

Purchasing, Selling Calls/Puts

There are four things you can do with alternatives:

1. Purchase calls
2. Sell calls
3. Purchase puts
4. Sell puts

Purchasing stock gives you an extended position. Purchasing call options give you a potential long view in the hidden share. Short-selling a stock gives you a short look. Selling a bare or revealed call gives you a possible short position in the underlying stock.

Purchasing a put alternative gives you a potential short position in the underlying stock. Selling a stripped, or unmarried, but gives you a possible long place in the hidden inventory. Keeping these four situations straight is significant.

Individuals who purchase options are called holders, and the individuals who sell options are called authors of options. Here is the important qualification among holders and authors:

1. Call holders and put holders (purchasers) are not committed to purchase or sell. They have the decision to practice their privileges. This restricts the danger of purchasers of alternatives to just the premium spent.

2. Call scholars and put authors (venders), in any case, are committed to purchase or sell if the alternative lapses in-the-cash (more on that underneath). This implies a merchant might be required to follow through on a guarantee to buy or sell. It additionally suggests that alternative dealers have an introduction to additional, and sometimes, boundless, dangers. This implies essayists can lose considerably more than the cost of the alternatives premium.

Theory

The theory is a bet on future value bearing. An examiner may think the cost of a stock will go up, maybe dependent on crucial examination or specialized investigation. An examiner may purchase the stock or buy a call alternative on the stock. Estimating with a call option—rather than buying the inventory inside and out—is alluring to specific dealers since options give influence. Out-of-the-cash call options may just cost a couple of dollars or even pennies contrasted with the maximum of a $100 stock.

Supporting

Alternatives were indeed concocted for supporting purposes. Supporting with other options is intended to decrease the chance at a sensible expense. Here, we can consider utilizing choices like a protection arrangement. Similarly, as you safeguard your home or vehicle, options can be used to protect your ventures against a downturn.

Envision that you need to purchase innovation stocks. Be that as it may, you likewise need to restrict misfortunes. By utilizing put options, you could limit your drawback chance and appreciate all the upside in a financially savvy way. For short dealers, call options can be used to confine misfortunes assuming incorrectly—particularly during a slight crush.

What is Options Trading?

At the point when the vast majority consider speculation, they consider purchasing stocks on the financial exchange, and many are presumably totally ignorant of terms like options exchanging. Buying shares and clutching them with the end goal of making long haul additions is one of the more typical venture systems. It's likewise a consummately reasonable to way contribute, giving you have some thought regarding which stocks you ought to purchase or utilize a facility that can offer you counsel and direction on such issues.

This methodology is known as a purchase and hold system and can enable you to expand your riches over the long haul, yet it doesn't give a lot, And when anything, in the method for transient increases. Nowadays, numerous speculators are utilizing a progressively dynamic venture style to attempt to make increasingly prompt returns.

On account of the scope of online handles that empower speculators to make exchanges on the stock trades with only a couple of snaps of their mouse, it's moderately direct for financial specialists to be progressively dynamic if they wish to. Numerous individuals exchange online on either low maintenance or a full-time premise, purchasing and selling consistently to attempt to exploit shorter-term value changes and frequently clutching their buys for only half a month or days, or even only several hours.

There are a lot of budgetary instruments that can be effectively exchanged. Options, specifically, have demonstrated to be extremely prevalent among merchants, and options trading is winding up increasingly standard. On this page, we have given some valuable data on what is associated with alternatives exchanging and how it functions.

Indeed, you've got it - alternatives exchanging is just exchanging options, and is commonly finished with protections on the stock or security advertise (only as ETFs and so forth).

First off, you can sell alternatives through a business-like E*Trade (ETFC) or Fidelity (FNF).

When purchasing a call alternatively, the strike cost of a possibility for a stock, for instance, will be resolved dependent on the present price of that stock. For example, if a portion of a given stock (like Amazon (AMZN) is $1,748, any strike value (cost of the call alternative) that is over that offer cost viewed as "out of the cash." Conversely, if the strike cost is under the present offer cost of the stock, it's considered "in cash."

In any case, for put options (appropriate to sell), the inverse is valid - with strike costs underneath the present offer value being considered "out of the cash" and the other way around. Furthermore, what's increasingly significant - any "out of the cash" alternatives (regardless of whether call or put options) are useless at lapse (so you genuinely need to have an "in cash" options when exchanging on the securities exchange).

Another approach to consider it is that call alternatives are commonly bullish, while put options are widely bearish.

Alternatives commonly lapse on Fridays with various periods (for instance, month to month, every other month, quarterly, and so on.). Numerous alternatives agreements are a half year.

How Options Work

As far as esteeming alternative agreements, it is basically about deciding the probabilities of future value occasions. The more probable something is to happen, the more costly an alternative would be that benefits from that occasion. For example, a call worth goes up as the stock (fundamental) goes up. It is the way to understanding the overall estimation of options.

The less time there is until expiry, the less worth an alternative will have. This is because the odds of value move in the underlying stock reduce as we move nearer to expiry. If you purchase a one-month choice that is out of the cash, and the stock doesn't move, the options turn out to be less significant as time passes. Since time is a part of the cost of an alternative, one-month options will be less critical than three-month options. This is because, with additional time accessible, the likelihood of a cost move in support of you increments, and the other way around.

Exchanging Call versus Put Options

Acquiring call options is wagering that the cost of the portion of security (like stock or record) will go up throughout a foreordained measure of time. For example, if you purchase a call option for Alphabet (GOOG) at, state, $1,500, and are feeling bullish about the stock, you are foreseeing that the offer cost for Alphabet will increment.

When buying put options, you are anticipating the cost of the underlying security to go down after some time (in this way, you're bearish on the stock). If you are obtaining put options on the S&P 500 record with a present estimation of $2,100 per share, you are bearish about the financial exchange. You are accepting the S&P 500 will decrease in an incentive over a given timeframe (possibly to sit at $1,700). For this situation, since you acquired the put options when the file was at $2,100 per share (accepting the strike cost was at or in cash), you would have the opportunity to sell the options at that equivalent cost (not the new, lower-cost). I would approach a decent "cha-ching" for you as a financial specialist.

Options exchanging (particularly in the financial exchange) are influenced fundamentally by the cost of the basic security, time until the termination of the options, and the instability of the basic security.

The premium of the options (its cost) is dictated by natural incentives in addition to its time esteem (extraneous worth).

Chronicled versus Suggested Volatility

Instability in options exchanging alludes to how huge the value swings are for a given stock.

Similarly, as you would envision, high instability with protections (like stocks) implies higher hazard - and alternately, low unpredictability means lower chance.

When exchanging options on the securities exchange, stocks with high unpredictability (ones whose offer costs sway a great deal) are more costly than those with low instability (albeit because of the whimsical idea of the financial exchange, even small instability stocks can turn out to be great unpredictability ones in the long run).

Why Use Options?

Recorded unpredictability is a decent proportion of instability since it quantifies how much a stock vacillated every day over a one-year timeframe. Then again, suggested uncertainty is an estimation of the unpredictability of a stock (or security) later on dependently available over the hour of the alternative agreement.

Worth: Time Value and in/at/out of the Money

And when you are purchasing an option that is as of now "in cash" (which means the alternative will quickly be in benefit), its exceptional will have an additional expense since you can sell it promptly for a profit. Then again, if you have an option that is "at the cash," the alternative is equivalent to the present stock cost. Also, as you may have speculated, a choice that is "out of the cash" is one that won't have extra worth since it is right now, not in benefit.

For call alternatives, "in cash" agreements will be those whose fundamental resource's value (stock,

ETF, and so forth.) is over the strike cost. For put options, the agreement will be "in cash" if the strike cost is beneath the present cost of the hidden resource (stock, ETF, and so on.).

The time esteem, which is likewise called the outward worth, is the estimation of the alternative over the intrinsic worth (or, over the "in the cash" region).

If an option (regardless of whether a put or call alternative) will be "out of the cash" by its termination date, you can offer options to gather a period premium.

The more extended an alternative has before its lapse date, the additional time it needs to make a benefit, so its top-notch (cost) will be higher because its time worth is higher. On the other hand, the less time an option agreement has before it lapses, the less its time worth will be (the less extra time worth will add to the premium).

In this way, as it were, if an option has a ton of time before it lapses, the more extra time worth will be added to the top-notch (cost) - and the less time it has before termination, the less time worth will be added to the premium.

Upsides and downsides

A portion of the significant masters of alternatives

exchanging spin around their alleged security

As per Nasdaq's alternatives exchanging tips, options are regularly stronger to changes (and downturns) in market costs, can help increment salary on present and future ventures can frequently improve bargains on an assortment of values and, maybe above all, can enable you to profit by that value rising or dropping after some time without putting resources into it legitimately.

There are cons to exchanging alternatives - including hazards.

There is an assortment of approaches to decipher dangers related to alternatives exchanging, yet these dangers spin around the degrees of unpredictability or vulnerability of the market. For instance, costly options are those whose vulnerability is high - which means the market is unpredictable for that specific resource, and it is progressively dangerous to exchange it.

Options Trading Strategies

When exchanging options, the agreements will ordinarily take this structure:

Stock ticker (name of the stock), date of termination (usually in mm/dd/yyyy, albeit in some cases times are flipped with the year first, month second and day last), the strike value, call or put, and the top-notch cost (for instance, $3). So a case of a call alternative for Apple stock would look something like this: APPL 01/15/2018 200 Call @ 3.

Contingent upon what stage you are exchanging on, the alternative exchange will look altogether different.

There are various techniques you can utilize when options were exchanging - all of which fluctuate on hazard, reward, and different elements. And keeping in mind that there are many procedures (the more significant part of them genuinely convoluted), here are a couple of structural systems that have been prescribed for apprentices.

Secured Call

And when you have great resource speculations (like stocks, for instance), a secured call is an incredible alternative for you. This system is commonly useful for speculators who are just nonpartisan or marginally bullish on a stock.

A secured call works by purchasing 100 portions of standard stock and selling one call option for every 100 shares of that stock. This sort of technique can help lessen the danger of your present stock speculations yet additionally gives you a chance to make benefit from the alternative.

Secured calls can profit when the stock cost increments or remains consistent over the hour of the options agreement. Be that as it may, you could lose cash with this sort of exchange if the stock value falls excessively (yet can in reality still profit And when it just falls a smidgen). In any case, by utilizing this technique, you are shielding your venture from reductions in offer cost while allowing yourself the chance to profit while the stock cost is level.

Selling Iron Condors

With this technique, the merchant's hazard can either be moderate or hazardous, relying upon their inclination (which is unmistakable in addition to). For iron condors, the situation of the exchange is non-directional, which means the advantage (like a stock) can either go up or down - along these lines, there is benefit potential for a genuinely wide range. To utilize this sort of system, sell a put and purchase another put at a lower strike cost (basically, a put spread), and consolidate it by buying a call and selling a call at a higher strike value (a call spread). These calls and puts are short.

At the point when the stock value remains between the two puts or calls, you make a benefit (along these lines, when the value changes to some degree, you're profiting). In any case, the procedure loses cash when the stock cost either increments definitely above or drop radically underneath the spreads. Therefore, the iron condor is viewed as an impartial market position.

Options Trading Examples

There are heaps of instances of alternatives exchanging that, to a great extent, rely upon which system you are utilizing. In any case, as a fundamental thought of what an ordinary call or put options would be, we should consider a broker purchasing a call and put an alternative on Microsoft (MSFT).

When you purchased a long call alternative (recollect, a call option is an agreement that gives you the privilege to buy shares later on) for 100 portions of Microsoft stock at $110 per share for December 1, you would reserve the option to purchase 100 pieces of that stock at $110 per share paying little respect to if the stock value changed or not by December 1. For this extended call options, you would expect the cost of Microsoft to increment, consequently giving you a chance to harvest the benefits when you can get it at a less expensive expense than its reasonable worth.

If you choose not to practice that privilege to purchase the offers, you will lose the top-notch you paid for the alternative since you aren't committed to buying any suggestions.

And when you were purchasing a since quite a while ago put options for Microsoft, you would wager that the cost of Microsoft offers would diminish up until your agreement terminates, so that, And whenever you practiced your entitlement to sell those offers, you'd sell them at a more significant expense than their reasonably estimated worth.

Another model includes purchasing a long call option for a $2 premium (so for the 100 offers for every agreement, that would rise to $200 for the entire deal). You purchase a possibility for 100 portions of Oracle (ORCL) at a strike cost of $40 per share, which lapses in two months, anticipating that stock should go to $50 at that point. You've burned through $200 on the agreement (the $2 premium occasions 100 offers for the contract). At the point when the stock value hits $50 as you wager it would, your call alternative to purchasing at $40 per offer will be $10 "in cash" (the agreement is presently worth $1,000 since you have 100 portions of the stock) - since the distinction somewhere in the range of 40 and 50 is 10. Now, you can practice your consider alternative and purchase the stock at $40 per share rather than the $50 it is currently worth - making your $200 unique agreement now worth $1,000 - which is an $800 benefit and a 400% return.

Basic Options Trading Mistakes

There are a lot of missteps; even prepared merchants can make when exchanging options.

One basic mix-up for merchants to make is that they think they have to clutch their call or put alternative until the termination date. If your options' underlying stock goes far up overnight (multiplying your request or put alternative's worth), you can practice the agreement promptly to procure the increases (regardless of whether you have, say, 29 days left for the options).

Another regular error for alternatives brokers (particularly fledglings) is to neglect to make a decent leave plan for your options. For instance, you might need to plan to leave your alternative when you either endure a misfortune or when you've arrived at a benefit that is just as you would prefer (rather than holding out in your agreement until the lapse date).

What does Option Trading Involve?

In fundamental terms, options exchanging includes purchasing and selling options contracts on the open trades and, extensively, it's fundamentally the same as the stock exchange. Though stock merchants expect to make benefits through purchasing stocks and selling them at a more significant expense, options dealers can make benefits through buying alternatives agreements and selling them at a more considerable expense. Likewise, similarly, that stockbrokers can take a short position on stock that they accept will go down in worth, options merchants can also do with alternatives contracts.

By and by, in any case, this type of exchange is more adaptable than stock exchanges. For a specific something, the way that options agreements can be founded on a wide assortment of fundamental protections implies that there is a lot of degree with regards to choosing how and where to contribute. Dealers can utilize alternatives to theorize on the value development of individual stocks, files, remote monetary forms, and items in addition to other things, and this introduces unmistakably more open doors for potential benefits.

The genuine flexibility, however, is in the different options types that can be exchanged.

When exchanging stocks, you fundamentally have two principle methods for profiting through taking either a long position or a short position on a particular stock. If you anticipated that a specific stock should go up in worth, at that point, you would take a long place by purchasing that stock with the end goal of selling it later at a more significant expense. If you anticipated that a specific stock should go down in worth, at that point, you would take a short position by short offering that stock with a want to repurchasing it later at a lower cost.

In alternatives exchanging, there's increasingly

decision in the manner in which exchanges can be executed and a lot more approaches to profit.

It ought to be clarified that options exchanging are a substantially more confounded subject than stock exchanges, and the entire idea of what is included can appear to be exceptionally overwhelming to amateurs. There is absolutely a great deal you ought to learn before you begin and contribute your cash. Notwithstanding, the majority of the essentials aren't that hard to understand. When you have gotten a handle on the nuts and bolts, it turns out to be a lot more clear precisely what alternatives exchanging is about.

Beneath, we clarify in more detail all the different procedures included.

Purchasing Options

Purchasing an option agreement is practically speaking indistinguishable to purchasing stock. You are essentially taking a long position on that options, anticipating that it should go up in worth. You can purchase alternatives shrinks by basically picking precisely what you wish to purchase and what number of, and afterward putting in purchase to open request with an agent. This request was named all things considered because you are opening a situation through purchasing alternatives.

If your options do go up in worth, at that point, you can either sell them or exercise your alternative relying upon what suits you best. We give more data on selling and practicing alternatives later.

One of the enormous focal points of options agreements is that you can get them in circumstances when you anticipate that the hidden resource should go up in worth and cases when you expect that the necessary resource should go down.

When anticipating that a hidden resource should go up in worth, at that point, you would purchase call options, which gives you the privilege to acquire the fundamental resource at a fixed cost. If you were anticipating that a vital resource should go down in worth, at that point, you would purchase put options, which gives you the privilege to sell the hidden support at a fixed cost. This is only one case of the adaptability on these agreements; there are a few more.

If you have recently opened a short position on options decreases by thinking of them, at that point, you can likewise repurchase those agreements to close that position. To close a situation by purchasing contracts, you would put in purchase to close requests with your intermediary.

Selling and Writing Options

There are mostly two manners by which you can sell alternatives contracts. Initially, if you have recently purchased agreements and wish to understand your benefits, or cut your misfortunes, at that point, you would offer them by putting in an offer to close request. The request has named all things considered because you are shutting your situation by selling alternatives contracts.

You would ordinarily utilize that request if the options you possessed had gone up in worth and you needed to take your benefits by then, or if the alternatives you claimed had fallen in value. You needed to leave your situation before bringing about some other misfortunes.

The other way you can sell options is by opening a short position and short selling them. This is otherwise called composition alternatives because the procedure includes you composing new agreements sold in the market. When you do this you are assuming the commitment in the contract for example and when the holder practices their options, at that point you would need to sell them the fundamental security at the strike cost (if a call options) or purchase the underlying security from them at the strike cost (if a put alternative).

Composing alternatives is finished by utilizing the offer to open requests, and you would get an installment at the hour of submitting such a request. This is commonly more hazardous than exchanging through purchasing and after that selling, yet there are benefits to be made And when you recognize what you are doing. You would as a rule put in such a request And whenever you accepted the applicable hidden security would not move so that the holder would have the option to practice their options for a benefit.

For instance, And whenever you accepted that a specific stock was going to either stay static or fall in worth, at that point, you could compose and sell call options dependent on that stock.

You would be obligated to potential misfortunes if the stock went up in worth, however, And when it neglected to do as such when the options terminated, you would keep the installment you got for thinking of them.

Practicing Options

Options dealers will, in general, make their benefits through the purchasing, selling, and composing of alternatives instead of ever really practicing them. Notwithstanding, contingent upon the procedures you are utilizing and the reasons you have purchased certain agreements, there might be events when you practice your alternatives to purchase or sell the hidden security.

The straightforward truth that you can conceivably make cash out of practicing just as purchasing and selling them further serves to represent exactly how much adaptability and flexibility this type of exchanging offers.

Options Spreads

What truly makes exchanging options such a fascinating method to contribute is the capacity to make alternatives spread. You can make cash transferring by purchasing options and after that selling them And when you make a benefit, yet the spreads are the genuinely amazing assets in exchange. A range is essentially when you enter a situation on at least two options agreements dependent on the equivalent fundamental security; for instance, purchasing alternatives on a particular stock and composing arrangements on a similar share.

There are various sorts of spreads that you can make, and they can be utilized for a wide range of reasons. Most regularly, they have utilized as far as possible the hazard associated with taking a position or decreasing the budgetary expense required with taking a position.

Most options exchanging systems include the utilization of spreads. A few methodologies can be exceptionally confused, yet there are additionally various genuinely essential techniques that are straightforward.

Step by step instructions to Buy And Sell Options

It is showcase shrewdness that keen alternative dealers purchase modest options and sell costly options. Furthermore, without a doubt, we often observe that the perfect alternative to purchasing will be very expensive (and in this way dangerous), regardless of the high likelihood of value development. Undoubtedly, the whole idea of secured call composing is worked around that center standard: selling overrated (exaggerated) options to the individuals who overlook this guideline.

Stock Price and Its Effect on Option Values

Since investment opportunities purchased to open all around are purchased to either hypothesize on the stock's development or to fence against the event, it is common that an option's worth will move because of changes in stock cost.

Call esteems move a similar way as the stock and put esteems move contrarily (inverse) to the stock cost. The measure of progress in an option's price will be controlled by the alternative's delta – clarified further on. One who thinks a stock will inescapably rise would purchase a call to conjecture on it; if bearish, a put would be the acquisition of decision.

Purchasing Options

Other than to close a short alternative position, brokers purchase investment opportunities for two essential reasons: to support a current stock position or to hypothesize on the course of the hidden stock. The individuals who anticipate that the stock should go down will purchase puts, either theoretically or fence a long stock position. The individuals who expect that the stock should go up will buy calls, either hypothetically or to a short area in the capital.

Since investment opportunities can be purchased for a small amount of the expense of the underlying stock, yet give the holder the privilege to acquire (calls) or sell (puts) the hidden share whenever through termination, they provide the holder influence over the basic offers for the life of the alternative.

Model: If you pay $100,000 for a six-month call alternative to purchase for $5,000,000, you control the particular thing for the options time frame, for an ostensible entirety. This is an influence. The proprietors of the business can't offer the property to any other person until your options lapses. You can practice the call whenever, sell the options or let it lapse – it's your decision. Unexercised, the request will terminate uselessly.

Theorizing on stock heading by buying alternatives is an old game, and it can work very well. The issue is that the stock must make the ideal move before termination. In this way, the purchaser of the option must get both the course and timing of the stock move right.

Selling Options

Dealers sell investment opportunities principally to create a salary. The system utilized will be managed by whether one is bullish/nonpartisan or bearish (list discards alternative spreads):

· Bullish/Neutral: offer secured calls to produce pay

· Time esteem premium produces returns in any event when the stock itself is level

· Bearish: sell calls bare to exploit stock's disappointment

· Releases exchange to termination or repurchases calls at a benefit when the stock pulls back

· Bullish/Neutral: sell OTM puts as an option in contrast to a secured call

· Exposed put composing makes a salary, the OTM strike lessens task chance

· Bullish: sell ATM, or even ITM puts into gaining stock at markdown

· The put premium lessens the stock expense whenever relegated; unadulterated benefit if not allowed

Purchasing Options – Strategy

Examiners purchase investment opportunities fundamentally to theorize on a foreseen development in the hidden stock since the options will pick up in an incentive as the stock moves. Examiners don't purchase options when they have a nonpartisan attitude toward the capital, so the technique utilized is directed by whether one is bullish or bearish.

Bullish: purchase calls to profit by the anticipated stock ascent

ITM call is most costly yet gains in cost at the most elevated rate with stock's ascent

ATM call is the best worth, however, doesn't move dollar-for-dollar with the stock

OTM call is least expensive yet factually the most exceedingly terrible purchase

Bearish: purchase puts into gaining by anticipated stock fall

ITM put is most costly yet gains in cost at the most noteworthy rate with stock's fall

ATM put is the best worth, however, doesn't move dollar-for-dollar with the stock

OTM put is least expensive yet factually the most noticeably awful purchase

If the options' value moves dollar-for-dollar with the stock, the options' delta is 1.0 for a call and - 1.0 for a put. If the alternative moves $0.50 for a dollar move in the stock, the delta is 0.50 for a call and - 0.50 for a put.

Consequently, for instance, when the stock is $45, the 50 Call may cost just $1.00, however with a delta of 0.30, the capital would need to move to about $53 altogether at the call cost to twofold. The stock needs to work a lot harder (move further) to make gainfulness for the ATM or OTM call purchaser. The additional time esteem the purchaser paid, the more the stock must move.

Not all ng alternatives are theoretical. Alternatives are likewise purchased to fence a contradicting position. For instance, one who is short the stock may buy a defensive call to guarantee the capacity to buy the stock at a true cost should the exchange turn out badly (stock goes up). Or then again, one who is long the capital may purchase a defensive put to guarantee the capacity to sell the stock at a real cost should the stock fall.

Time Value

It is essential for anybody composing secured calls or making any alternative based exchanges to comprehend time worth and its significance. For the alternative author, time worth is one of the significant wellsprings of return (the other benefits from sharply exchanging options as the stock moves). In any case, for the alternative holder, time worth is harmful since it rots and picks his pocket over the long haul. Altogether for along options situation to win, the purchaser of the option initially should recover the time an incentive before the exchange can end up productive. For instance, if when the stock is $50, the broker pays $2 for the present 50 Call, which is ATM, and therefore unsurpassed worth, the breakeven point is $52 (50.00 strike cost + 2.00-time esteem). The holder must consider selling the stock for $52 to recover the calls' expense, and just the sum got above $52 will be gain.

It is regularly said that time is the options author's companion and the alternative purchaser's foe. This is valid because time worth rots at an anticipated rate as time slips by.

Time Value in Short Calls

In the secured call, returns produced when a worth bit of the premium. Accept that we purchased a stock for $50 and composed the 45 Call on it for a $6.00 dividend. That is a hefty premium, yet we are committed to selling the stock for $45 whenever called. The time worth is just $1.00 (6.00 − 5.00 of inherent worth).

Whenever got out at $45, our benefit will be the $1.00 of time esteem, in spite of that tremendous call premium, since we are selling the stock at a $5.00 misfortune.

Time Value in Long Options – and How It Is Forfeited

Assume that as opposed to purchasing the stock, we had bought the 45 Call at the expense of $6.00. The call gives us the privilege to buy the stock – presently exchanging at $50 – for $45. Deducting out the $5.00 of special incentive from the calls' cost, we paid $1.00 in time esteem. Be that as it may, if the call instead is worked out, the time worth is discarded.

This exchange would bring about a $1.00 misfortune. By practicing the call, the holder relinquishes the time esteem. Time and incentive for the holder of the option genuinely is a "utilization it or lose it" suggestion. At whatever point an ITM call or put has time esteem, the holder relinquishes the time an incentive upon exercise. Had the alternative holder rather sold the calls for $6, the time worth would have been recovered? In any event, marketing the calls for $5.50 would have yielded a superior outcome than relinquishing all the time esteem.

The main route for the alternative holder to recover the calls' time worth is to sell the options, and the closer lapse draws near, the additional time worth will rot. This outlines why ITM calls are not practiced before termination since, despite everything, they have time esteem. However, when time worth is gone or almost gone, it is never again an obstacle to early call practice, and the call essayist can confront new tasks whenever. If the call exchanges beneath equality (underneath inherent worth), the first exercise turns out to be much almost certain.

Guessing on stock bearing by acquiring alternatives is an old game, and it can work very well. The issue is that the stock must make the ideal move before lapse.

Bullish: sell ATM or even ITM puts to procure stock at rebate

The put premium lessens the stock expense whenever allowed; unadulterated benefit if not relegated.

Purchasing Options – Strategy

Examiners purchase investment opportunities principally to estimate on a foreseen development in the underlying stock since the options will pick up in an incentive as the stock moves. Theorists don't purchase alternatives when they have an impartial attitude toward the capital, so the methodology utilized is directed by whether one is bullish or bearish.

Bullish: purchase calls to profit by the anticipated stock ascent

ITM call is most costly yet gains in cost at a most noteworthy rate with stock's ascent

ATM call is the best worth, yet doesn't move dollar-for-dollar with the stock

OTM call is least expensive however factually the most noticeably awful purchase

Bearish: purchase puts to benefit from anticipated stock fall

ITM put is most costly yet gains in cost at the most elevated rate with stock's fall

ATM put is the best worth, yet doesn't move dollar-for-dollar with the stock

OTM put is least expensive yet factually the most noticeably terrible purchase

And when the options' value moves dollar-for-dollar with the stock, the alternative's delta is 1.0 for a call and - 1.0 for a put. If the option moves $0.50 for a dollar move in the stock, the delta is 0.50 for a call and - 0.50 for a put.

Hence for instance, when the stock is $45, the 50 Call may cost just $1.00, yet with a delta of 0.30, the capital would need to move to about $53 altogether at the call cost to twofold. The stock needs to work a lot harder (push further) to make a benefit for the ATM or OTM call purchaser. The additional time esteem the purchaser paid, the more the stock must move.

Long Option Economics

Here is a significant point about the financial matters of purchasing alternatives: eventually, the holder of the option should either sell or exercise the ITM extended options. Something else, the options will lapse useless. Accept as in the above model that an author paid $6.00 for a $45 consider when the stock is $50. If the holder makes no move by termination, the calls will lapse useless, bringing about the loss of the whole premium paid. And when the stock still is at $50 when lapse moves around, instead of assuming a $6.00 misfortune, the holder could practice the 45 Call to purchase the stock for $45 and sell it at $50, which decreases the disaster to $1.00, as appeared in the time-esteem relinquishment model above.

And when the stock has stayed at $50, at that point near termination the call holder could roll the shouts to the following month by selling the present require its $5 of special incentive in addition to any outstanding time worth and purchasing the next month's 45 Call for around $6. The expense of the roll would be an extra $1 or so of time esteem (really, the distinction among present and one month from now time an incentive for the calls), however, rolling the gets out keeps the broker in the game and abstains from relinquishing the calls' true worth. Rather than assuming a $1.00 misfortune, at that point, the merchant could instead utilize the equivalent $1.00 to roll the gets out one month.

OTM options are never practiced even at termination since it would be unquestionably progressively profitable to purchase or sell the stock at the market.

Futures:

Tips for putting resources into securities exchange - Trading prospects

And when you don't here is a snappy definition, a future is a kind of auxiliary instrument where two gatherings consent to execute a lot of budgetary tools or physical wares for future conveyance at a specific cost.

Here is a more straightforward clarification, suppose you choose to purchase a link membership. You are the purchaser in this model; you go into a concurrence with the link organization to get specific help to a particular cost for the following year. This is like a fates contract; you have consented to get an item at a future date at a specific price and specific terms. You have verified the cost for the present, and regardless of whether the value rises and by going into this agreement, you have discounted your danger of more significant expenses.

The fates market has numerous dangers. However, the possibility to make enormous benefits is significant because of a lot of instability in these business sectors. There is a wide range of prospects markets and systems you can use in them, they are.

Items

Items are physical items whose worth is controlled by market interest. These can incorporate gold, grains, and vitality. One methodology you can use in these business sectors is "Straddles." A straddle is built by holding a similar number of calls (where you guess that the cost will rise) and puts (where you conjecture that the price will fall) with the same strike cost and termination date. The fundamental thought is that you figure the costs will stay unpredictable later on, either going up or down.

Another technique is to purchase a call choice, buy calls when you accept that the cost of the advantage will acknowledge sooner rather than later. Then again, you will obtain a put choice if you take the price will decrease.

Monetary forms

At the point when you exchange monetary standards, you conjecture that the costs of money will rise or fall later on. One methodology utilized is called scalping; this is the point at which you endeavor to make momentary benefits from the gradual changes in the estimation of cash. And when you do this, again and again, you will, in the end, make noteworthy benefits.

Files and loan fees

Timing systems are amazingly famous in these business sectors; double-crossing procedures utilized are cycle and regular exchanging.

Cycle exchanging is finished by examining the recorded date and discovering conceivable here and there cycles for an essential resource. Usually utilized cycles for stock list prospects are the multi-week and multi-day period. Examining the value patterns related to cycles can prompt massive additions for shrewd speculators.

Occasional exchange is the point at which you endeavor to transfer the regular impacts that happen in these business sectors. Verifiable information shows that most markets have comparative examples of a seemingly endless amount of time after year. Thinking about these random patterns is a powerful method to exchange for the benefit.

Another excellent method to begin is by focusing on these four distinct fates showcases; this will fabricate your insight as you learn without expanding your general measure of hazard; at that point, as you incorporate certainty extends with exchanging different sorts of fates.

Futures are investments that allow you to buy commodities by locking in a certain price at a specific time without actually buying the shares. These are speculative bets you are placing on the future price of a commodity, sometimes far in advance. In addition to products such as crude oil and corn, stocks, foreign currencies, and Treasury bonds are also connected to futures and can be traded on various exchanges.

On the one hand, a distinct advantage of locking in a price for an extended period is to mitigate some of the volatility in a particular market. On the other hand, making short-term bets on an increase in price can yield massive returns. Because there are unlimited gains and unlimited losses, this type of investment is typically recommended for savvy and aggressive investors who have extremely high tolerance levels for risk. The examples of investors who use futures generally include hedge funds, wealthy individual investors, and institutions.

With futures contracts, you do not own the shares or the actual commodity. You don't even put down the same amount as if you were purchasing the asset. What is most appealing about futures is the opportunity to gain from short-term shifts in the price of the commodity either based on the movement of the market, often hedging against significant losses in markets that tend to experience more volatility. Despite the risks that accompany futures, most experts agree that they are a reliable diversification tool in addition to, and with different characteristics than stocks and bonds. As a result, they are rapidly growing in popularity with individual investors.

If you are getting your feet wet in futures markets, the first thing you will want to do is to open an account with a broker at a reputable trading firm. Select a futures market that is active easy to liquidate. You will then be required to put down a margin. While you can open an account at a brokerage with just a few thousand dollars, you will need to place a much more significant chunk of cash into a futures trading account to cover any margin calls should the price of the commodity drop. This is needed to cover losses to maintain the minimum amount of funds required as part of your contract.

Individuals can trade their accounts without a broker. This approach increases the risk and requires constant care and attention to trends and predictions. A managed account allows your broker to leverage their expertise and trade on your behalf, reducing the amount of time, concentration, and some degree of risk for you. A third option is to select a commodity pool — that pools together a set of commodities. The benefits of commodity pools are similar to that of mutual funds in that they pool together funds from several investors, investing in several products. These also don't require margin calls. However, the general risks that are inherent in other types of futures trading still exist with commodity pools.

If you are beginning to learn about futures, why not do some paper trades first? Pretend to buy, hold, and sell to see if you come out ahead in the game. This simulation may prevent you from losing lots of real money!

ETFs:

A trade exchanged reserve (ETF) is a sort of security that includes a gathering of protections, for example, stocks—that frequently tracks a hidden list, even though they can put resources into any number of industry divisions or utilize different techniques. ETFs are from numerous points of view like common assets; be that as it may, they are recorded on trades, and ETF offers an exchange for the day only like standard stock.

Kinds of ETFs

There are different kinds of ETFs accessible to financial specialists that can be utilized for money age, hypothesis, cost increments, and to the fence or mostly counterbalance hazard in a speculator's portfolio. The following are a few instances of the kinds of ETFs.

Security ETFs may incorporate government securities, corporate securities, and state and neighborhood securities—called municipal securities.

Industry ETFs track a specific industry, for example, innovation, banking, or the oil and gas segment.

Product ETFs put resources into items, including unrefined petroleum or gold.

Money ETFs put resources into extreme monetary

forms, for example, the Euro or Canadian dollar.

Backward ETFs endeavor to win gains from stock decreases by shorting stocks. Shorting is selling a stock, anticipating a decline in esteem, and repurchasing it at a lower cost.

Financial specialists ought to know that numerous backward ETFs are Exchange Traded Notes (ETNs) and false ETFs. An ETN is a bond yet exchanges like a stock and is upheld by a backer like a bank. Make sure to check with your intermediary to decide whether an ETN is a correct fit for your portfolio.

In the U.S., most ETFs are set up as open-finished assets. They are dependent upon the Investment Company Act of 1940 except where the following guidelines have changed their administrative prerequisites. Open-end assets don't restrain the number of speculators associated with the item.

Step by step instructions to Buy and Sell ETFs

ETFs exchange through online intermediaries and customary intermediary sellers.

You can see a portion of the top specialists in the business for ETFs with Investopedia's rundown of the best agents for ETFs. An option in contrast to standard dealers is Robo-counsels like Betterment and Wealthfront who utilize ETFs in their speculation items.

Preferences and Disadvantages of ETFs

ETFs, give lower ordinary expenses since it would be costly for a financial specialist to purchase every one of the stocks held in an ETF portfolio exclusively. Financial specialists need to execute one exchange to buy and one transaction for selling, which prompts less intermediary commissions since there are just a couple of exchanges being finished by speculators. Representatives usually charge a commission for each trade. A few agents even offer no-commission exchanging on absolute ease ETFs diminishing expenses for financial specialists significantly further.

An ETF's cost proportion is the expense to work and deal with the store. ETFs commonly have low costs since they track a file. For instance, if an ETF tracks the S&P 500 record, it may contain each of the 500 stocks from the S&P, making it an inactively overseen reserve and less time-escalated. Be that as it may, not all ETFs track a record in an inactive way.

Creation

At the point when an ETF needs to give special offers, the A.P. purchases portions of the stocks from the record, for example, the S&P 500 followed by the store—and sells or trades them to the ETF for new ETF shares at an equivalent worth. Like this, the A.P. sells the ETF partakes in the market for a benefit. The procedure of A.P. offering stocks to the ETF support, as a byproduct of offers in the ETF, is called creation.

The most common errors not to commit

Stay away from These Common Mistakes When Investing In ETFs

ETFs, which are crates of stocks, securities, or products that are exchanged on a stock trade, is turning into an undeniably mainstream approach to contribute particularly with youthful speculators. Because of their availability, moment expansion, straightforwardness, low costs, charge proficiency, and capacity to be exchanged like individual stocks, a few specialists even think they'll, in the end, make customary common supports out of date.

In any case, there are drawbacks to know about as well. And when you have ever heard the saying "your most prominent quality can be your shortcoming also," at that point, you will perceive any reason why the accompanying errors can crawl up on an ETF financial specialist if they don't know about them.

Misstep: not changing how you contribute your cash

Numerous individuals put by storing a set sum into their speculation account each month (dollar-cost averaging methodology), which they use to purchase common assets. This can be a slip-up with ETFs since you pay a commission for each purchase and sale request you place which implies that commission costs will diminish your month to month speculation. (Note: this could be discredited And when you are with an online business firm that gives free exchanges.)

Slip-up: losing the focal point of your long haul methodology

ETFs are, for the most part, seen as a long haul speculation holding. Still, since of the advantage of having the option to exchange it (as regularly as intra-day), an error could be made if the financial specialist gets enticed to purchase and undercut with all the more a term viewpoint (read: showcase timing) which can bring about selling at an inappropriate time and having higher exchanging costs and duties.

Misstep: not looking into how an ETF differentiates your portfolio

This can neutralize you in two different ways:

Repetition. For instance, by putting resources into an ETF that tracks the S&P 500 and holding an enormous top shared reserve, you are putting resources into basically a similar sort of stock, and customarily the two speculations will hold similar organizations.

Liquidity danger of specific ETFs. The other miscue is if your ETF is put resources into a particular segment, for instance, in an Antarctic oil sands benchmark (I'm developing a portion), you may experience issues selling your offers when you need.

Mix-up: exchanging "over your head."

"Because a procedure exists doesn't mean you have to utilize it."

One of the benefits of putting resources into ETFs is the adaptability of how they are exchanged and the various methodologies that can be utilized. For instance, one procedure is to "short-sell" an ETF. This methodology is utilized by speculators who accept the cost of their ETF will go down. The speculator, as a result, obtains shares from the business firm, and after that will compensation back the acquired offers with the less expensive offers – expecting the cost does in actuality go down.

Sounds simple right? Not a chance! This is a training that lone experienced speculators may utilize and keeping in mind that the reward (a better yield) could be decent; the hazard is extremely high.

Great guideline affirming principle: in light of the fact that a system exists doesn't really mean you have to utilize it.

At long last, if you inevitably choose to put resources into ETFs, by and large, it's best when you have a singular amount to contribute as that will help limit exchanging costs (see botch 1). Numerous ETFs will have low least speculation prerequisites (could be as low as $250) yet be cautious; an exceptionally low least venture may require a month to month stores, which, as a result of commission expenses, could consume your general return.

Real Estate:

The land is mainstream speculation. There are numerous alterations in the financial framework having puffed-up hazard or lesser returns; the commercial venture center goes on with the arrangement innovative and attractive thinking draws near. These advancements make it significant for land licenses to have necessary and cutting-edge information on land ventures. This doesn't imply that licenses should go about as venture guides. For all the time, they ought to allude speculators to proficient assessment bookkeepers, lawyers, or venture experts. These are the experts who can offer master guidance on a financial specialist's particular needs.

Investing in Real Estate: Factors to consider

The three variables of putting resources into land are region, discernment, and financial aspects. The way to making the best interest in and, and explicitly in cooperatives, and townhouses, is to consider all the three variables. Putting resources into land compare to specific duties concerning the buyer. Interest in the ground made exclusively upon the area of the property won't yield those outcomes. Before making speculation, it is essential to incorporate the three contemplations

o Consider in general zone.

o Consider familiarity with the zone.

o Consider the budgetary components.

Real Estate Investment: Benefits

Land esteems have fluctuated widely in different regions of the nation. However, numerous land speculations have appeared better than expected paces of return, for the most part, more noteworthy than the predominant financing costs charged by contract loan specialists. In suspicion, this implies the financial specialist can use the impact of leased cash to contribute a land buy and feel relatively sure that, whenever held long enough, the benefit will yield more money than it cost to fund the buy.

The land offers financial specialists more prominent power over their ventures than make different choices, for example, stocks and so on. Land financial specialists, likewise, are given guaranteed expense focal points.

The most common errors not to commit in real estate

1. Detach Between Real Estate Decisions and Overall Business Strategy

The most significant thing you should remember when occupied with a business land choice is that the choice you are making isn't about land, it's about your business. You're not renting/buying space—you're developing your business.

The greatest mix-up made by little and mid-showcase organizations is the inability to completely adjust and associate land choices within the general business procedure. Indeed, even organizations with as meager as 2,500 sq. Ft. of space can increase noteworthy operational, money related, and promoting focal points by adopting a key strategy.

2. Inability to Understand the Market

With the Internet today, it is simpler than any time in recent memory to think you have a comprehension of the market. In only seconds you can perceive what space is accessible and even how much space is renting or selling for.

This has had two adverse outcomes:

Outfitted with this data, entrepreneurs and administrators have been hushed into a misguided feeling of certainty.

Furthermore, land merchants have gotten self-satisfied. It's simpler than any time in recent memory to force reams of information, print out huge amounts of pictures, and present the presence of learning. While this has helped realtors close business, it's stinging their customers.

3. Mistaking Direct Costs for Total Cost of Occupancy

It appears to be basic enough; include your yearly lease/contract installments, include any form out, and include the expense of utilities and upkeep. When you include these variables, you discover the space that meets your requirements and has the least "cost." As with most business standards, what seems straightforward and clear is normally not successful.

Bonds:

When putting resources into relationships, it's essential to:

Realize when bonds develop. The development date is the date when your speculation will be reimbursed to you. Before you submit your assets, realize to what extent your thinking will be tied up in the bond.

Know the bond's appraising. A relationship's evaluating means that how financially sound it is. The lower the rating, the more hazard there is that the bond will default – and you lose your speculation. AAA is the most noteworthy rating (utilizing the Standard and Poor's appraising framework). Any relationship with a grade of C or beneath is viewed as low quality or garbage bond and has the most noteworthy danger of default.

Examine the bond guarantor's reputation. Knowing the foundation of an organization can be useful when choosing whether to put resources into their bonds.

Comprehend your resistance for the chance. Securities with a lower FICO score commonly offer a better return to make up for more elevated levels of hazard. Ponder your hazard resistance and abstain from contributing exclusively dependent on yield.

The three significant kinds of securities are corporate, metropolitan, and Treasury securities:

Corporate securities are obligation instruments given by an organization to raise capital for activities like extension, innovative work. The premium you win from corporate securities is assessable. Be that as it may, corporate securities usually offer better returns than government or civil securities to balance this drawback.

Municipal securities are given by a city, town, or state to fund-raise for open tasks, for example, schools, streets, and emergency clinics. In contrast to corporate securities, the premium you procure from city securities is tax-exempt. There are two kinds of city bonds: general commitment and income.

CONCLUSION

In any case, a sizeable extent of the rest of forex exchanging is theoretical with merchants working up speculation, which they wish to sell at some phase for benefit. While money may increment or diminish in worth comparative with a broad scope of monetary standards, all forex exchanging exchanges depend on cash sets. In this way, the Euro might be 'solid' against a bushel of financial standards, and merchants will trade only one money pair and may worry about the Euro/U.S. Dollar (EUR/USD) proportion. The changes in relative estimations of monetary standards might be slow or activated by explicit situations, for example, are developing at the hour of composing this - the poisonous obligation emergency.

With straddles (long in this model), you as a dealer are anticipating the advantage (like a stock) to be profoundly unpredictable; however, don't have the foggiest idea about the bearing wherein it will go (up or down). When utilizing a straddle system, you, as the merchant, are purchasing a call and put options at a similar strike cost, hidden cost, and expiry date. This system is regularly utilized when a broker is anticipating the supply of a specific organization to plunge or skyrocket, generally following an occasion like an income report. For instance, when an organization like Apple (AAPL) is preparing to discharge their second from last quarter income on July 31st, An option merchant could utilize a straddle system to purchase a call options to terminate on that date at the present Apple stock cost, and furthermore purchase a put options to lapse around the same time at a similar price.

For chokes (long in this model), a speculator will purchase an "out of the cash" call, and an "out of the cash" put all the while for a similar expiry date for the equivalent essential resource. Financial specialists who utilize this system are accepting the fundamental support (like a stock) will have an emotional value development; however, they don't know in which heading. What causes a long to choke a to some degree safe exchange is that the financial specialist needs the stock to move more noteworthy than the all-out premium paid, yet it doesn't make a difference where bearing.

The upside of a choke procedure is that there is less danger of misfortune since the premiums are more affordable because of how the options are "out of the cash" - which means they're less expensive to purchase.

CPSIA information can be obtained
at www.ICGtesting.com
Printed in the USA
LVHW050523120121
676187LV00006B/314